KRAMBAMBULI

Copyright © 2018 Syr Ruus

Except for the use of short passages for review purposes, no part of this book may be reproduced, in part or in whole, or transmitted in any form or by any means, electronically or mechanically, including photocopying, recording, or any information or storage retrieval system, without prior permission in writing from the publisher or a licence from the Canadian Copyright Collective Agency (Access Copyright).

Published in Canada by
Inanna Publications and Education Inc.
210 Founders College, York University
4700 Keele Street, Toronto, Ontario M3J 1P3
Telephone: (416) 736-5356 Fax (416) 736-5765
Email: inanna.publications@inanna.ca Website: www.inanna.ca

We gratefully acknowledge the support of the Canada Council for the Arts and the Ontario Arts Council for our publishing program. We also acknowledge the financial support of the Government of Canada.

Printed and Bound in Canada.

Cover design: Val Fullard

Library and Archives Canada Cataloguing in Publication

Ruus, Syr, author
    Krambambuli / Syr Ruus.

Issued in print and electronic formats.
ISBN 978-1-77133-573-7 (softcover).-- ISBN 978-1-77133-574-4 (epub).--
ISBN 978-1-77133-575-1 (Kindle).-- ISBN 978-1-77133-576-8 (pdf)

    1. Ruus, Syr. 2. Ruus, Syr--Childhood and youth. 3. Ruus, Syr--Family. 4. Authors, Canadian (English)--Biography. 5. Refugees--Estonia--Biography. 6. Refugees--Germany--Biography. 7. Refugees--Austria--Biography. 8. Immigrants--United States--Biography. 9. Immigrants--Canada--Biography. I. Title.

PS8635.U96Z465 2018   C818'.603   C2018-904376-8
                                                                                 C2018-904377-6

KRAMBAMBULI

A MEMOIR BY

SYR RUUS

Memoir Series

*For every person
who has been displaced by war.*

Krambambuli—
The finest brew
To ever foam inside a glass.
Is that so?
We ought to know!
That's why we sing
Krambambuli.
KRAM-BIM-BAM-BAMBULI
KRAM BAM BU LI

—Seventeenth-century German
drinking song translated from
the Estonian by the author

Overture

MY MOTHER, EMA, PURSES HER LIPS and waggles her head at me in irritation. She is eighty-two. I am fifty-six.

Perfumed and powdered, with her hair styled into a smooth grey bob and her well-manicured fingernails a more subdued shade than I remember, she is cloaked in a silk ensemble of large pink roses. *A flower among flowers*, she jokes, smiling five-thousand-dollar bridgework. A gallery is showing twenty-seven of her most recent watercolours. "Lilacs" has already sold before the official opening. She is pleased with herself. And with good reason. Ema is a survivor, able to skim graciously over the surface of life by eliminating the past, refusing to speak of it, and, with luck, never thinking about it either. "Can't you remember anything pleasant about when you were a child?" she asks.

Yes, Ema, I do remember. And so I write...

I am cutting out pictures from a discarded newspaper to serve as paper dolls. It is difficult to find a photograph with all the limbs intact. Often parts of arms are gone and both legs are missing from the knees down. The photos are mostly of grown-ups; children are harder to find. I press the cut-outs carefully, like fragile flowers, between the pages of an old copybook I have labeled HOCHFELD 237, AUGSBURG, DEUTSCHLAND. This was our address in the Displaced Persons Camp where we lived from 1946 to 1949, before we came to America. I call it my *tenement book*.

Newsprint is scarce, not a scrap wasted. You bring home whatever you can scavenge and allow me to cut out pictures before tearing the pages into small squares for the WC and demonstrate how to prepare the paper by rubbing it hard between the knuckles until it becomes soft enough for wiping.

I play paper dolls with my friend, Helle. She has some with all the limbs intact that she cut from an old fashion magazine. Somewhere, she even found a baby. My best dolls are: General Eisenhower wearing lots of medals on his chest with both arms and both legs, missing only his feet; the top halves of the Sun Maid Twins cut from the sides of the small box of raisins we got in a Red Cross package; and, best of all, Princess Elizabeth and Prince Philip, both intact and wearing their wedding outfits, which took up most of the newspaper's front page on November 21, 1947. I use a tiny folded scrap of light blue paper for their baby, pretending that he is wrapped in a blanket, and give them three pages of my HOCHFELD book to live in because they are royalty.

Helle is nine, older than me. She has chapped lips and a constant sniffle, even in summer, and lank brown hair that she chews on out of habit. She knows a lot about grown-ups and thinks up most of our games. We remove our dolls from their rooms between the pages of our tenement copybooks and pretend they attend choir practice or to go to the theatre or to parties. They also have fights and secrets and love affairs.

Helle and her mother live in the building next to ours, in a bigger room with three other women who stay up late at night smoking *paberossi* and playing cards. Her mother has a green eye and a brown one, but Helle's are both grey with droopy lids, probably because she never shuts them so as not to miss anything that's going on even when she's supposed to be asleep. The men in her building make liquor in the cellar, and have parties where everyone gets drunk. You go there too, Ema. Do you remember? And you come back foolish. You lie in bed sick all the next day. Never again, you promise.

We are lucky to be in a room with just the two of us, you say, but I think Helle is luckier. She has more fun. Helle tells me that a man at her place kisses her and tickles her and lies down with her on her bed when no one else is around. He is in love with her, she says. He is eighteen. A grown-up.

In our unit, we share the kitchen and WC with an old couple who lives in the other small room across the hallway and with four young men in the large room next door. They were soldiers in the war like my father, Isa. Three are maimed, missing arms or legs. One is funny in the head. Whenever they are able to get liquor, they stay up all night, yelling or singing sad songs about the lost homeland. Afterward there is often vomit in the WC or in the hallway. I am supposed to stay away from them.

You don't like Helle either, I can tell. You would rather have me play with Annie-Mannie because you and Tädi Leena, Annie's mother, are best friends. Tädi Leena has a tapeworm that lives in her stomach, and, whatever she eats, the worm gets most of it. We only have the little white worms. Everyone has those, you say.

Annie is not yet seven and doesn't know a lot of grown up stuff like Helle. She has a father and an older brother who is almost a man. Her mother calls her Annie-Mannie. We all make fun of her. *Annie-Mannie! Annie-Mannie! Time to come in now,* we taunt, and Annie goes home, crying. She is spoiled and tattles about everything.

Annie and I play paper dolls too, but not with cut-out people doing real-life things like with Helle. There is an older girl in Annie's building who draws really well, and if we nag her long enough she makes dolls for us with her set of coloured pencils. When you and Tädi Leena get together to lay out cards for double solitaire, Annie and I draw dresses for these dolls, adding little tabs at the shoulders and waist and cutting slits in the hats so they stay on.

To celebrate Annie-Mannie's seventh birthday, you convince Tädi Leena that we should all go sunbathing since it has turned out to be such a lovely day. You have heard of the perfect spot, you say. You are always finding things to do and places to go, holding my hand to take me along. *An energetic woman*, I overhear someone say. I suspect that means something bad so I don't tell you what I heard.

Were you pretty when you were young? I wonder now. You sometimes wore silk stockings and lipstick, kept your long brown hair curled, your fingernails filed and painted. You were certainly much better looking than Tädi Leena. Even with her tapeworm and when there was hardly enough food to fill anyone's belly, Tädi Leena already looked like a fat woman waiting to emerge, plodding beside you, my energetic mother, while Annie and I skip along the sidewalk down the whole length of Hochfeld Strasse, past the Estonian sector and through the parts occupied by foreigners—Latvians and Lithuanians—until the paved road ends and the fields take over.

After that we see no one. We remove our shoes to feel the sandy earth between our toes like at Piirita Beach back in Estonia, where we went sometimes in the summer when I was little. There, women were allowed to take off all their clothes to sunbathe within a boarded enclosure called *Naiste Paradiis*. The fence was drilled full of holes by the men and boys who lurked about outside so they could peek in.

Pfui! Men are disgusting. Remember that, Totsu! you warned me even then.

Annie and I pick the wildflowers which grow abundantly along the edges of the path, gathering huge bouquets of fragile red poppies, white daisies, and blue cornflowers. It is quite a distance to our destination, and Annie has begun to whine when we spot the rusting hulks of war machinery rising up from the golden field of wheat. Turrets and cannons. Rusted tanks. The burnt out, mangled remains of airplanes. Anti-aircraft guns, most of them damaged, but some still able to spin like merry-go-rounds. An amusement park left over for the children of the survivors. Large craters pockmark the landscape. We slip down into the depths of one of the deepest bomb holes where no one can see us. Already the surface has been reclaimed by tender blades of sweet-smelling grass.

"Much more private than the Women's Paradise at Piirita Beach," Tädi Leena chuckles, pulling off her blouse to release large white breasts veined in blue.

You and Tädi Leena stretch out side by side on the blanket. Annie and I keep our clothes on, since we aren't interested in sunbathing. After outlining your pale naked bodies with the wildflowers we have gathered, we clamber out to explore the fascinating playground up above.

Spinning wildly on the hulks of anti-aircraft machinery. Sitting in burnt-out cockpits, pretending to fly in the rusting remains of planes shot from the sky. Sliding down the shiny wings. Climbing to the tops of huge rubber tires. Hanging by our knees from the barrel of a cannon. Straddling the rough metal turrets of machine guns, causing bright red welts to appear on our tender thighs. So involved in our play, we never notice a stranger is watching.

Annie sees him first and pulls at me to hide.

"Shhhh," she says. "Look!"

I peer out to where she is pointing.

A scraggly-looking man sits with his back against a derelict howitzer, cradling on his naked belly a swollen purplish growth that he rubs with his hand.

"*Pfui!*" I make a face. "That's disgusting."

I duck back into our hiding place, but the man has seen me, for when I look again, he smiles and gives a jolly little wave.

"What is it?" I whisper, clutching at Annie. "What's that huge purple thing?"

"You know," Annie says, snickering.

I don't know, but I realize that this must be some sort of a game, for each time we peek out, the man smiles and waves, continuing to rub more vigorously, which causes us to collapse into uncontrollable giggles. It all seems so silly, but daring too, tinged with forbidden danger—certainly nothing we should reveal to our mothers. Still, after a while, even this gets boring. Besides, Tädi Leena has brought a special birthday lunch and we're hungry, so we leave him sitting there and run back to the bomb hole.

Weeks later Annie-Mannie tattles.

"Why didn't you tell us right away?" you gasp, shielding your breasts with one arm and grabbing my shoulder tightly with the other as you fix upon me your piercing blue gaze.

First I feel wronged.

Then I feel guilty.

Why didn't I tell you?

Because I saw something I wasn't supposed to see.

"*Pfui!*" Ema sniffs after she reads what I have written. "Why must you write such filth? You always remember the bad things.

I much prefer to surround myself with beauty."

She's right, of course. Beauty is easier on the eye than truth.

It was only after we passed through the Resettlement Center on our way to a different life in a new world that I started to become aware that my childhood was not as happy as I had formerly assumed. We were Displaced Persons. We were damaged and deprived. We had to find sponsors to guarantee us jobs and endured months of screening to ascertain that we were mentally and physically fit enough to start our lives anew as productive members of society in a better place.

For many years, I denied my past and attempted to become somebody else, adapting to the language, the rules, and the nuances of a different culture. We started at zero, but we were survivors. With patience and hard work, it was possible to achieve one's dreams in this new land. Yet, for a long while, something was missing.

Beauty truly is in the eye of the beholder.

For me it is the unique life in its entirety that I have come to treasure as my own.

PART I
REFUGEES

1.
Ema

EMA GREW UP IN TALLINN, Estonia's capital city, during the heady days of the new independence.

I envision her as an earnest, dutiful child with long, thick braids, a conscientious student eager to achieve and ambitious to advance her status. She would be respectful of her mother, but disdainful also, for though Memme knew how to read and write and was gaining a reputation as a dressmaker, she had come from the country and, in her daughter's opinion, was slow to adapt to modern, urban ways.

It was 1928 and Ema was fifteen. After 700 years of servitude to foreign powers, empowered by a strong sense of nationalism and confident of a glorious future, the younger generation no longer concerned itself with the years of hopeless oppression. Times were still hard, but they would get better. Among a gaggle of girls in their grey school uniforms, dark woollen stockings, and green neckerchiefs, Ema headed homeward from the *Gümnaasium* through the narrow medieval streets. They huddled together, giggling, as boys from the nearby technical school shouted taunts. When a farm wagon clattered by, its huge iron-bound wheels loud on the cobblestones, the girls shrieked at the top of their voices in joyful abandon, embarrassed when the road changed suddenly to asphalt and only their voices remained reverberating in the air.

As they passed the *Fotografia* Studio on Narva Avenue, they stopped to stare at one particular photograph displayed in the store window. His torso was bare, his hands encased in boxing gloves, his muscular arms raised to strike an imaginary foe, his dark hair tousled wild with a few errant locks hanging down into his blazing eyes. *Ooh Volli! Ahh Volli!* The girls could hardly contain themselves. He was the best looking man they had ever seen.

Ema kept her silence, concealing a secret smile. For the past two months, she had spent every Friday evening in the same room with this paragon of masculinity at chorus practice. She had been stealing glances at him where he stood, taller than most in the back row of the bass section. He was much older than she—twenty-one— and a student at the University of Tartu. He must have taken note of her too, for just last week he had asked if he could walk her home.

For the entire three blocks, trudging along beside him on wooden feet, staring straight ahead, Ema could think of nothing to say. But it didn't bother Volli that he did all the talking for he was filled to the brim with nationalistic fervour. Estonian men were the bravest in battle; Estonian language was the most melodious in the world, with a grammar so complex that it was nearly impossible for any foreigner to learn; Estonian maidens were unsurpassed in their physical beauty and the gentleness of their hearts.

Not knowing how to take her departure when they arrived at her door, she stood in silence, shifting from one foot to another, desperate to use the bathroom. "Finally I just peed into my boot," she admitted as she told me the story of their courtship. "I was wearing my long winter coat. He never noticed a thing and continued right on talking."

She didn't see him again until several months later and couldn't recall a single word he had said that night. But she hadn't forgotten Volli.

From a young age, Volli possessed charm, dash, and charisma. He was a patriot, a freedom fighter, and a handsome and sensitive intellectual given to writing poetry. He was also an orphan, all alone in the world. To tell a good story, he exaggerated his accomplishments and enlarged his emotions for his audience— his valour, his ardour, his grief. A room came alive when Volli entered. He had a knack for getting women to feel sorry for him. No one could resist him.

No one that is, except Ema. It was important for her to maintain self-control and even when young, she guarded her innermost feelings. This only served to increase the intensity of his pursuit.

The most time they ever spent together was before they were married. During the short northern summers, they would often take the tram from Tallinn to Piirita Beach to swim, to play volleyball, or to have a cool drink and dance on the Pavilion while the orchestra played Strauss waltzes. Volli was an avid sportsman and gymnast. He fenced, he boxed, and he liked to show off his physical prowess on the beach by doing innumerable push-ups, standing on his head, or walking on his hands, to the delighted admiration of the young girls gathered around him.

During the long, dark, snowy winters, they joined a folk-dancing troupe, walked in Kadriorg Park, and went cross-country skiing. Always there was singing. Folk songs. Love songs. Drinking songs. Patriotic songs praising the Estonian landscape, lamenting the years of oppression, glorifying the fight for freedom. *My Fatherland, my luck, my joy, how beautiful thou art*, the national anthem, was sung at every public occasion. Wherever Estonians gathered, voices raised up in song. Groups of singers practised in villages and towns throughout the land in preparation for the National Song Festival held every summer in the large stadium built especially for this purpose on the outskirts of Tallinn. There would be a grand parade through the city with the participants dressed in the unique national costumes representing their particular county. Ema and Volli marched among the rest.

For six years he courted her. Although there were many other women eager for his attentions, she was his port in the storm, his anchor, his solace, the only one in the world who really understood him. Without her, he claimed, he'd die. His ardour finally overcame her reservations, and when she turned twenty-one, she consented to be his wife. By then, she had cut off her braids, graduated from Commercial College and was earning a salary. She felt sorry for him. She thought she could change his ways and introduce some stability into his life.

They rented a small flat on the third floor of an old house on Herring Street. With her usual energy, Ema redecorated—sewing curtains, embroidering pillows for the sofa, arranging flowers for the table. There was no kitchen. She would prepare gourmet meals on a hot plate with two burners, searching for special recipes and keeping everything warm for her husband's arrival. But Volli preferred his potatoes and meat cold and was much too involved in the political ideas that surged about in his brain to take notice of her domestic endeavours. Intense about the broad perspective, he never concerned himself with details. He was impulsive, funny, a prankster. He liked to show off, joke around, and feel important. She was responsible and organized. She took care of the practical aspects of their existence. She was no longer laughing. She had grown up. She began to think of him as childish, immature. A typical man.

Once men get what they want, it's all over, she would tell me even before I was old enough to understand.

Volli had a passionate nature. During their prolonged, intermittent courtship, he kept hoping for her to succumb, but Ema remained firm in her convictions, and no amount of persuasion would induce her to relent. Upon their marriage, it is possible they were both disappointed in their expectations.

"Sex, *pfui*," Ema scoffed the one time I was bold enough to ask. "We got married and after some years you were born."

The euphoria of the new independence didn't last long either. Estonian men were known to be stubborn and proud. They liked to sing patriotic songs, to drink vodka and schnapps, and to engage in political debate. Factions arose almost immediately, yelling loudly at each other across the cobblestones of the ancient city without anyone properly hearing what was being said. Volli became active in a right-wing dissident group which attempted to seize power from the provisional government. Many of its most vocal members, Volli among them, were convicted of treason against the new Republic of Estonia and subsequently imprisoned. After spending only one winter on Herring Street as a married couple, Volli went to jail and Ema moved back home to live with Memme.

She was allowed a monthly visit. She would make up a package of food and wait all day in the line-up at the prison gate. More often than not, she would be informed that due to insubordinate behaviour Volli was once again in solitary confinement and was allowed no visitors. *If everything is taken from you, pride becomes the only recourse,* he would say in his own defence. When Ema retold this tale years later, it was to evoke sympathy for herself, but it was my father I felt sorry for.

After the government of the Independent Estonian Republic was officially established four years later, the political prisoners were released. Ema, Memme, and Volli moved into an apartment together on Rosencrantz Avenue in the centre of the city, close to the architectural firm where Ema worked as a bookkeeper. I was born the following winter—the year World War II began. The Republic of Estonia immediately declared itself neutral, but it was only a matter of months before Soviet forces invaded and disbanded the newly elected government. Over thirty thousand Estonian men (my uncle Ossi among them) were mobilized to serve in labour battalions in Northern Russia. Intellectuals, business leaders, and all those suspected of anti-Communist activities were rounded up in the middle of the night to be transported to Siberia. There the conditions were so harsh that most did not survive.

What made this time so unbearable, Ema revealed later, more than the lack of food and the poverty, was the paranoia. To improve their own lives, people informed on others. If you happened to remark that the price of eggs was too high, your neighbour might report you to the authorities. Even in your own home, you weren't safe. In school, children were coaxed to tell what their parents talked about behind closed doors. Because of his political views, Volli was well aware of the danger. Whether to save himself, to protect his family, to fight for his beliefs, or possibly for all these reasons, he joined a resistance group, the Forest Brethren, and spent the years of the first Communist occupation somewhere in the back country practising the techniques of guerrilla warfare.

War often becomes a matter of choices and chances, guardian angels and horrifying repercussions. When the Germans returned two years later, many regarded them as liberators from the hated Russian regime. Neutrality, though declared, was no longer an option. Estonian troops who had fought with the Russians in the first war to drive out the Germans, now joined with Hitler's army to defend the homeland against the return of Communist rule. Volli came out of hiding and wore the Estonian uniform. I was three years old. I didn't remember him. I didn't know him. I was afraid of him. My father, Volli—my Isa.

For a while, life became more tolerable for some, though not for the seven thousand Estonians who were executed for collaborating with the enemy, nor for the minority groups—the Jews and the Romany—who were eliminated or placed in Nazi concentration camps.

2.
12 Rosencrantz Avenue

If YOU HAD A CHOICE, which animal would you be? my mother asks.

A Turtle, I say. *You carry your house on your back and tuck in your head for safety.*

But they're so slow, she replies. *I'd much rather be free as a bird.*

Always we remained opposites

I say what I think, Ema said.

I mostly kept my mouth shut in a pout so as not to offend by disagreeing. During my first seventeen years, when I lived with my mother, and for a long time afterward, two individuals vied for dominance inside my soul—the outwardly agreeable and the inwardly resentful—neither one expressing my true nature. Accordingly, I had three names: *Totsu*, when I was good, *Tita* when I was bad, and the one that appeared on the official documents.

Be a good girl, Totsu, and fetch me my purse.

Pull up your socks, don't slouch, and stop biting your fingernails. You really are a Tita.

My mother was a perfectionist, and, despite the huge catastrophe which had disrupted her life, she refused to tolerate small deficiencies in her pursuit of an orderly and cultured existence.

You played a wrong note.

You should copy that over.

You can do better, Tita. That doesn't look nice. Here, let me show you how.

She was of a generation that believed that humiliation built character, that children should be seen and not heard (unless performing), that all discipline was for their own good, and that they should be forever grateful to their parents. When I was little there was always a willow switch in full view on top of the closet door for punishment, a common practice at the time, though I cannot remember her ever using it. For me, shame was sufficient.

Häbi, häbi Tita, she would scold, twirling her manicured forefinger at my face as I swelled with disgust at myself. It never took long for *Totsu* to vanish and for *Tita* to take her place. The merest hint of disapproval would bring on the sulk.

"You never had a real home," Ema sighs in a rare moment of personal reflection. "That's why you've turned out to be so...."

"Neither do millions of other oppressed children all over the world as long as wars continue," I interrupt, bristling as usual whenever the topic of my negative personality comes up for its annual review.

It is 1965. I am twenty-six. Ema is fifty-two. I am an instructor in the English Department of a Midwestern university and have just arrived for my yearly visit. We are watching the news about yet another war, this time in Vietnam. There have been student demonstrations. To the cheers of the crowd, an agile, bearded youth climbs a flagpole in an attempt to pull down the American flag.

Pfui! my mother exhales loudly, spreading her talons. "I could tear that man apart with my fingernails."

How many women and children did we kill or maim today? I muse quietly, biting my lip as Ema leans forward for the attack.

"We have to stop the spread of Communism or they'll take over the world. You of all people should know that. They insinuate themselves everywhere. They've infiltrated the news media, the films, university campuses. Don't you realize that Communist propaganda is behind all these riots? Have you ever participated in any anti-war demonstrations yourself?" she demands, pointing her forefinger at me.

"I've never carried a placard, if that's what you mean."

"I can't believe it, Tita. You are so naïve."

It always ends up like this—as a personal attack. I don't respond.

"Oh, so now I've hurt your feelings. I'm sorry if I offended you, but, as you know, I'm a person who speaks her mind," she offers by way of apology. "I suppose you've tried marijuana too?" She releases a long, exasperated sigh as if my presence here on Earth is just another one of life's great disappointments she has to endure.

I am done with talking and take my sulk to the bathroom, feeling angry and immature, still not able to cope with this familiar conflict. Especially in Estonian, which she insists we speak whenever we're together so I will never forget my native language. I have formulated my opinions in English. I have hardly spoken Estonian to anyone except her since childhood. In my native language, I can only express myself in the words of a ten-year-old.

"Don't pout," she tells me. "You've always been overly sensitive and have never been able to accept criticism."

Perhaps.

But I did have a home. I remember it well: *12 Rosencrantz Avenue, Tallinn, Estonia.*

Our apartment was in a three-storey building constructed from large grey stones. We lived on the ground floor. I was allowed to go out the front door and down the three broad steps by myself to the courtyard in back. There, shaded by tall trees, was a grassy area containing a sandbox, where I would bake sand cakes and dig tunnels, while Memme kept an eye on me from the kitchen window up above.

We were far from wealthy, but our subsequent poverty enhanced my earliest memories with the sheen of affluence: the parquet floor, a shiny red cupboard with a tall mirror in the hallway, the Persian carpet hung on the wall behind the brown velvet sofa in the living room, the piano with gleaming ivory keys, the glass-fronted bookcases, vases of fresh flowers on polished tables, a large radio with a multitude of knobs in the corner. Tiny people lived in there who talked a lot about the war and sometimes played music. One time the radioman said: *And now for the little girl who's been waiting ... here's 'Lili Marlene' just for you.* I knew they had seen me even if I couldn't see them. It was my favourite song.

My toys were kept in the spare room where Memme slept—a dollhouse filled with tiny furniture; a prancing white hobby horse carved from wood with its long straw tail; the special big doll I wasn't old enough to play with yet and was only allowed to hold when I performed in the kindergarten show. I wore the dark red velvet dress with a big lace collar that Memme made for me on her sewing machine and sang "Me and My Dolly" in my loudest voice. Memme sewed for all of us. Ema wore a dress of the same bright flowered material as Dolly.

My mother was much more elegant than Memme. Her brown hair was curled with a permanent wave. Her fingernails and lips were painted a dark shade of pink. Her legs were encased in slippery silk stockings, and her shoes had high heels. Six days a week she went to work in an architectural firm.

Memme took care of me. Her hair was grey, cut straight and short like mine. She wore a long dark skirt covered over with an apron that she took off whenever we went outdoors. Her sewing machine stood in the corner of the dining room. I liked it when she pushed the treadle with her feet to make the wheel whir around and a needle jump up and down very fast creating tiny stitches. She gave me the leftover scraps so I could I play wash day. In a small enamel bowl filled with real water I would scrub each piece and hang it up to dry on the string Memme had wound around the legs of dining room chairs, upended for the occasion.

I was five when my mother and I left Estonia.

Only upon the death of Stalin in 1953 did the Iron Curtain part just enough to allow a trickle of communication to pass through from the West. Letters were censored, recipients' names recorded. Many were afraid to write and thus put their relatives in danger. Ema decided to take a chance. She sent a letter to Memme at 12 Rosencrantz Avenue in Tallinn to tell her that she and I had survived the war and were now living in the United States.

Miraculously, Memme was still alive also. As was Ema's brother, Ossi, who had somehow managed to make his way back from Siberia to Tallinn. He was now married with two daughters and all of them lived together in our former apartment at Rosencrantz Avenue. When restrictions became less harsh, they sent some old photographs, including several of me as a baby, one of Isa posturing in shorts and boxing gloves, a group-shot of cross-country skiers laughing in a snow bank, and a formal family portrait of a man and woman with three children.

"Who are these?" I ask when Ema shows me the photos.

"That's me." She points to a little girl in blonde pigtails, wearing an anxious expression and clutching the hem of her dress as she stands beside a woman, I take to be Memme.

"And that's my father and my mother and my sister and my brother."

"I didn't know you had a sister,"

"She died of diphtheria."

I study the photograph.

The father, my grandfather, is dapper and small, with neatly combed dark hair and a full moustache, dressed in a three-piece black suit, white shirt and tie, with a pocket-watch dangling by a chain upon his chest. At his side. an ample, full-breasted woman with bovine features and startled eyes, her copious light brown hair piled like a crown on top of her head—my grandmother, but not as I remember her. Both of them sit straight and stiff on hard-backed wooden chairs. The man's delicate fingers rest on his trousered knees; the woman's much larger hand holds a toddler on her lap. A young boy, my Onu Ossi, with cropped hair, wearing short pants, a matching tunic and dark stockings, stands next to his father. Although he is quite a bit taller, he has the same features as Ema. The two girls are decked out in white long-sleeved dresses, trimmed in lace. The only one of the group who doesn't look apprehensive is the little one, gazing with curious interest at the photographer, her expression innocent and open. In her face I see my own, before I became frightened of the world.

"Her name was Alide. She died when I was five," Ema says.

"You never told me anything about your life in Estonia when you were a child."

"You never seemed interested in your heritage," she replies. But then she decides to continue.

"We lived on Narva Avenue. My mother was a seamstress. My father left us when I was very young. Life was hard. I wanted to take piano lessons, but we were too poor. I didn't get along with my brother. We had different friends. He liked to drink.

He was conscripted by the Russians and taken to Siberia. I don't remember. I don't want to think about those times."

We left our homeland with two suitcases. We have no photo albums, no treasured mementoes, no scrapbooks filled with yellowed indications of past achievements. All the old stories are told only by ourselves and, like well-known fairy tales, repeated so often that they have lost their meaning. Our former lives are gone, destroyed, *kaput*.

Of my father's background, I know nothing. All Ema told me is that his mother owned a store and he was orphaned at a young age. "Didn't you ask him?" I persist "Didn't you ever wonder about his family, where he came from, what happened to his mother and father, how they died, what kind of people they were?"

"He was who he was. Lots of people died. Times were different then. We didn't talk about things like that."

Yet, though I know nothing of it, my father's ancestry too is within me and my children, and a part of the generations yet to come. The great horde of the dead is present in every one of us, a miniscule particle clamouring for existence, an ancient human voice still here to be heard if we would only listen:

We are of the same sinews and blood.

The beauty of every living being shines only for a moment.

It is possible that my toys still exist there among strangers in that faraway medieval city of Tallinn—the dollhouse, the rocking horse, the big beautiful doll in the bright, flowered dress sewn by my grandmother. Antiques now. Belonging to others who are unaware of my memories beyond the oceans of time and space. Or perhaps used up by Onu Ossi's children. Though we have never met, we are connected like cells in an organism, like planets in a galaxy, joined by our DNA, related in our humanity.

I too could have died when I was three, like my mother's baby sister Alide. I was playing with my collection of postcards on Rosencrantz Avenue, laying them out neatly side by side on the kitchen table, when a sickness came over me and I lay down on my bed. Then the hallucinations began: a fierce lion with an enormous mane. "His whiskers, his whiskers!" I screamed to Memme who sat by my side holding my hand. "Get away!"

The doctor said it was meningitis, and even if I was strong enough to survive the high fever, I would sustain severe brain damage.

Fortunately, what I had was double pneumonia, and I recovered quite speedily without noticeable damage. But the precariousness of life was firmly etched into my consciousness at a very young age. Memme made me recite my prayers at night, to which I would add my own: *Please protect us from ...*, each time thinking up new and more terrifying images until the list became so long that I feared I might omit the very thing that would get us.

"You were always a frightened child," Ema says. "High strung."

What did you expect? I think. But I don't say anything, prepared to spare her the pain of past recollections. She was afraid too, she reveals, but she has always striven to overcome fear by strength of will and a belief that a guardian angel is watching over her.

"Our personalities are just so different," she adds. "You keep everything to yourself."

How can I explain to her that this is the only way I know how to stop from disappearing entirely? She is so intent to burrow into my brain that if I let down my guard she will root up anything which could possibly germinate there that she hasn't planted herself. Like an insidious weed, I refuse to surrender the core of my being. And for that I feel guilty.

I admit that I was timid, apprehensive even of my own father when, after the Germans took control, he occasionally appeared for a few days at our apartment on Rosencrantz Avenue. *Stalin, Pfui*, I learned to say, to his delight. *A soldier's daughter*, Isa called me, and put me through trials to test my valour. He coaxed me to walk across the narrow top of a towering wall. He made me fall straight and stiffly backwards, catching me in his large hands only a few centimetres before my head hit the floor. He taught me to box, squatting on his heels, daring me to knock him over. *KRAMBAMBULI!* he would shout, tossing me high into the air. *A brave heart is a powerful weapon.*

In the evenings, he read aloud to my mother as I lay between them on their wide bed upon the flowery bedspread. I listened and watched the small black marks on the page transform into words in Isa's mouth. It was when I began to realize that books contained all of life's experiences without threatening me in any way that I began to read on my own.

Though I tried hard to appear brave to please my father, I was overpowered by a terrible dread most of the time. When left alone, even for a minute, I hid under a blanket, hoping that if any Communists came they would dismiss me as a pile of dirty laundry. At the sandbox, other kids would tease me by howling like an air raid siren, and I would run inside, bawling. In kindergarten, I was the youngest and was sometimes pinched and bullied. Every night Memme sat beside my bed and held my hand until I fell asleep. Although I was soothed by her presence, she frightened me even more with her stories from the Bible. *Only a few footprints of mankind will be left in the world, and the Chinese shall inherit the Earth,* she prophesied.

During air raids, I would sit in Memme's lap enfolded in her voluminous black skirt and listen to her pray. Almost every night, the sirens wailed their horrible warning followed by the subsequent roar of airplanes up above, the *pop-pop-popping* of anti-aircraft artillery and the whistle of bombs falling out of the sky until they exploded somewhere in the city. There was the sharp splintering of glass and the loud screaming of a child, who may have been me. *Hush, hush,* someone said, *if you hear the explosion, you're all right.* Finally, Ema decided that Memme and I should stay with relatives in the country where it was safer. She had to remain in Tallinn because of her job. She would visit on Sundays.

3.
Memme

MEMME WAS HOME.
Isa was a handsome stranger in a uniform.
Ema was a special treat.

Ema dressed me up in pretty dresses. She fluffed up my fine blonde hair and tied a big bow on top. Whenever we went anywhere together, I would flirt with strangers on the tram cars and in restaurants. *What a cutie! Just look at those dimples,* they would remark as Ema hugged me to herself and called me Totsu.

During the summers, we spent many Sundays at Piirita Beach. I loved carrying the water from the ocean in my tin bucket and pouring it into the holes I dug in the sand to watch it disappear. Ema and I would collect little shells, swing in the big chair swing, and take off all our clothes in Naiste Paradiis to lie naked in the sun. Later we would have cold drinks at the fancy Pavilion where an orchestra played. I'd always beg Ema to request my other favourite song, "When Mickey Mouse Went Out to Sea."

For that little blue-eyed Missie over there, the bandleader would announce, and I was permitted to get off my chair to dance. Everyone clapped for me when it was over. I could tell Ema was pleased.

Memme never came to the beach with us. She stayed at 12 Rosencrantz Avenue, cooking, cleaning, sewing, and reading the Bible. She stuck my hair behind my ears and made sure my face and hands were clean, that I finished everything on my plate, that my undershirt was tucked in and my clothes were tidy. She watched over me when I played. She taught me my prayers and held my hand every night so I could fall asleep.

Because of the Communist occupation, I had never received a proper church christening as a baby. This upset Memme greatly, for she believed I wouldn't be allowed into Heaven when I died. Because Death constantly hovered over us with its sharpened scythe, Ema finally agreed to arrange for a baptism even though I was already four years old. Memme spent a lot of time sewing a beautiful floor-length christening dress for me—white with little blue dots, puffy sleeves, and a pink velvet bow. A photographer came to take a commemorative picture some days before the actual event. Ema was still at work, so it was left to Memme to get me ready. She put on my special dress, stuck my hair behind my ears, wiped my face with a damp cloth, and handed me a few dried-up flower stalks from the vase on the dining room table.

When Ema saw the resulting photograph, she was furious. She said Memme should have known better than to give me those dead flowers to hold. At the very least she could have combed my hair and coaxed me to smile. Memme came from the country and wasn't smart or pretty like my mother. It was obvious to me then that Ema was the one really in charge.

Because of the bombings, Memme and I left Tallinn to stay at a farm where it was safer. Since she had to work, my mother stayed behind. Everything was different in the country. Memme and I slept together off the kitchen in a narrow bed covered with a blanket which Tädi Ulvi, the farmwife, had woven on a loom that took up an entire room bigger than ours. Water came in a bucket from a well in the front yard. The toilet was out in back. I missed my home on Rosencrantz Avenue. I missed the polished furniture and the mirror in the hallway where I admired myself as I danced and sang and practised making frightful faces. I wanted my books and my toys. I was scared of the bees and snakes and stinging nettles, and I didn't like the way Tädi Ulvi boiled potatoes without peeling them first.

Onu Joosep and Tädi Ulvi no longer had children themselves because their sons had been taken away by the war, but they invited the neighbour boys to come and play with me. Priit was six, and Imbu was eight. They both wore short pants held up by suspenders and had dirty knees. I could tell they thought I was stupid. They acted rough, punching and pushing each other for no reason, and said words I was never supposed to say—*kurat* and *sitt*. They told me the brown circles in the field were cow cakes and I should taste one, but Memme had already warned me not to touch them. Imbu dared Priit to eat some dried-up horse dung from the middle of the road, and he did. I wanted to show off too, so I put my feet and legs into the sleeves of my coat and said "Look what I can do?" Then I couldn't get them back out. The boys laughed and dragged me by the coattails across the pasture until I finally came loose. "Bet your arse is some bright red now," Imbu snickered. I went to Memme, crying. I didn't even know I had an arse.

On rainy days, we played inside. The boys showed me how easy it was to catch flies on the windowpane. We cupped them into our hands, pulled off their wings and had horse races, watching them crawl up the glass to see whose horse got to the top first. I felt bad after, thinking about what we had done. But if I said how the poor flies must have suffered, everyone would just laugh at me. Ribbons of yellow flypaper hung from the kitchen ceiling. Flies would get stuck there, buzzing and struggling to free themselves until they died. No one cared about that, not even Memme.

I didn't like the farm animals either—the cows with their horns, the horses with their enormous yellow teeth, the huge snorting pigs, the big dog with his loud bark. It was our job, Memme's and mine, to go to the henhouse each morning to collect eggs. I was afraid of the hens' pecky beaks and terrified of the noisy rooster who guarded them. Even the cats frightened me, rubbing against my legs. No matter how soft the fur, I was always conscious of the sharp claws. Besides the animals, the barn also housed a slatted wooden farm wagon and a shiny black open carriage with bright red leather upholstery. There I would sit, pretending I was a fairy-tale princess being driven back to 12 Rosencrantz Avenue by six galloping white horses.

On many nights, we heard the roar of airplanes passing overhead. Soon after, the muted detonations began, and the skyline of Tallinn lit up with a fiery glow. Memme prayed out loud to the Heavenly Father to protect her daughter and together we said *Amen*.

During most days, Memme and I worked picking berries: strawberries, raspberries, blueberries, red currants, black currants, gooseberries, foxberries. We brought our full containers to Tädi Ulvi, and she boiled the berries into jam. In the late afternoon, Tädi Ulvi would take me with her to the pasture to drive the cows home for the milking. She held my hand, and we both carried willow switches as we walked along the grassy lane behind the placid herd. There was always a pleasant smell of hay and manure in the barn. I would watch as she sat on a round stool and pulled at the udders to make white, frothy, warm milk stream into the bucket that she held between her knees. One time she called me over to sit on her lap so I could try, but nothing came out no matter how hard I squeezed. There was a trick to it, she said.

I saw Onu Joosep only in the evenings. After finishing the farm work, he would use water from the bucket to wash up in the kitchen sink before supper. Afterwards he sat down in a soft chair and smoked his pipe. He never said much, but he taught me to make knots and also how to tie my shoelaces in a perfect bow, both loops exactly the same.

Every Saturday evening my mother came by train and walked the five kilometres up the dusty road from the station to the farm. Memme and I always went to meet her. When we saw her coming, a small dot in the distance, we slowed our steps so it wouldn't be such a long walk back, and she quickened hers. Soon we could see her waving. She wore her brown walking shoes, her blue slacks, and a knitted sweater. On Sunday, after lunch, she would go away again. When she left, I was glad for things to get back to normal.

One morning in September, we heard the sound of a motor and noticed a cloud of dust coming closer very fast. A soldier on a motorcycle with a sidecar attached pulled into the farmyard. It was Isa, wearing his grey uniform and his jaunty cap. He had come to take me back to Tallinn. He had borrowed the motorcycle from his unit, and he said we had to leave immediately. An emergency, he called it.

In a rush, Memme dressed me in my sweater and coat. Isa settled me into the leather seat of the sidecar and covered me with a blanket. He stepped on a lever, and the motor gave a loud roar. This was even more thrilling than being driven back to the city by six white horses. I smiled and waved a jolly goodbye to Memme and to the others gathered in the yard. Imbu and Priit were staring with their mouths open. It was the last time I ever saw any of them.

Speeding down the dirt road, sitting next to this dashing soldier who was my father, I was too excited to be frightened. When we reached the pavement, we passed long lines of trucks and lots of men in uniform walking. Later I learned that these were the German troops leaving Estonia. They were losing the war. The Soviet army was advancing toward the West. Tens of thousands left everything behind and fled: from Estonia, from Latvia, from Lithuania, from the Ukraine, from Poland. They had all suffered under the Communist occupation a few years before. They had sided with the Germans against Russia. There would be repercussions.

We were fleeing too. My father's Estonian unit was merging with the German army, and my mother and I were going by boat to Sweden. Without Memme. She was too old, they said. They told me she didn't want to come with us, that she was afraid to leave her homeland and face an unknown future. I knew they were lying. There was room for only one passenger on the motorcycle.

That same night my father went back to his battalion, and Ema and I left 12 Rosencrantz Avenue with our two suitcases, crowded in the back of an open truck with others from the architectural firm. As I sat in the cold wind in the unfamiliar lap of my mother, I forgot Memme. It was Ema I clung to now.

Many decades later, I think of her again. My grandmother. Only now do I begin to feel her as a part of myself. Her indomitable spirit that led her from the farm to the city as a young woman, newly married. Her hard work and intelligence that enabled her to survive the First World War, to provide for her family, to build up a successful business, employing others to sew from the patterns she created. But I am also of my grandfather, a dreamy, unambitious man who liked to tinker, who no longer had a place in his wife's world, who wandered away long before I was born.

With his dapper moustache, his golden watch and chain.

   Dear Memme, I am so glad that you remained in the country with your relatives instead of being left all alone at 12 Rosencrantz Avenue in that apartment full of the beautiful polished furniture I remember. That when your daughter took her child and fled her homeland forever, your son, Ossi, was able to return to Tallinn and, finding the apartment empty, to move in. That he brought you back from the village to the city to live with him after he married and had children whom you cared for and who later cared for you. That you had a family who laid you out and washed you and dressed you in your best clothes as was still the custom in that deprived land, and buried you when you were well past eighty. I am sorry I never wrote to you after letters were finally permitted to cross the Soviet barrier and we each found out that the other was still alive. I was sixteen then and too preoccupied with my new life in America to consider you. Perhaps you never thought of me either. But somehow I doubt that.

4.
Escape

IN 1944, WHEN THE GERMAN forces began to retreat, it was the great and futile hope of most Estonians that the Allies would ensure the provisions of the 1934 treaty, which guaranteed independence to the Baltic States. As this was not to be, there was a desperate rush to flee before the oncoming Soviet surge. The director of the architectural firm where Ema worked, Härra Liiva, orchestrated our escape and made arrangements for the departure. But, like everyone else, he waited until the last possible moment. If my father hadn't come "to rescue me through enemy lines" as he told me later, I would have been left behind. Did Isa briefly desert his unit and steal a motorcycle to save his little daughter?

"I don't remember," Ema says. When I persist, she brushes me off. "That was probably just one of his big stories. I don't like to think about those days."

During the retreat, the seaport of Tallinn was extremely dangerous. Hr. Liiva hired a truck to transport us to the boat he had hired to take his family and his employees to Sweden. Ema was thirty-one. I was five. What was she thinking as she departed from the city of her birth, not only leaving family, friends, home, and possessions, but all her hopes, dreams, and expectations as well? Sitting on a suitcase in the back of an open truck with her little daughter asleep in her arms, speeding through the starlit night to face a future of unknown deprivations, she trusted in her guardian angel. And surely she must have felt some comfort being among her colleagues: the director, Hr. Liiva; her boss, Hr. Tamm; and the two young interns, Hr. Leps and Hr. Raud. In their company, along with their wives and children, Ema was not alone. Perhaps there was something else as well. I can only speculate, but I have no doubt that the secret bond between Gusti Tamm and my mother had already been established before this dark journey took us into exile.

Although times were hard, Ema had always liked her job. The architects she worked with were graduates of the Estonian university in Tartu and had studied in Germany to receive advanced degrees from the University of Heidelberg. They were cosmopolitan and debonair. They had managed to elevate themselves from the common lot of Estonian peasantry earlier than most. Even during the war, they drank cognac and smoked cigarettes. My father's pretensions and enthusiasms must have paled in comparison with these men. Besides, she saw her husband so rarely.

On workday afternoons, it became customary for the architects to meet their clients in the Tea Room across the street from the office, which flourished during the brief time of Nazi occupation and specialized in fine pastries, rich tortes, and Neapolitans served with coffee, tea, or a bottle of white Rhine wine. Often Ema was invited to join them. The Tea Dance had become a popular attraction. A small orchestra performed familiar Viennese waltzes as well as some of the newer music—the fox-trot, the tango, the rumba: "Moonlight Serenade," "Begin the Beguine," "Besame Mucho."

Dancing was almost an art form in those days. Although a partner was essential, there was very little bodily contact—his left hand on the small of her back, his right hand barely touching hers. A whiff of perfume. An errant lock of hair brushing a cheek. Eyes meeting and not turning away. A woman had to respond to a man's slightest signal to capture his particular rhythm, to feel it in her hips and surrender her body so they could precisely synchronize the movement of their feet.

Gusti Tamm was an excellent dancer.

The boat that was to take us to Sweden never arrived. Later we learned it was bombed and sunk *en route*. The Soviet forces had already entered Tallinn, and we remained stuck in an outpost. In desperation, young Hr. Raud, an experienced yachtsman, hired a small vessel from a local fisherman, determined to cross the Gulf to Finland with his pregnant wife. But the rough September seas soon put a stop to that. The boat capsized not too far from shore. I saw two dark shapes struggling to emerge from the black waves. It was not a dream; it was a memory.

The only option remaining was to obtain passage on a German military transport. There happened to be one anchored offshore, ready to join the convoy of ships that had departed from Tallinn the day before. The Germans willingly took along everyone who wanted to go. It seemed like a gesture of goodwill, but in actuality refugees were needed to bolster the labour force. As we headed out on a fishing boat for boarding, plumes of black smoke began to rise from the immense ship. Like ants from a disturbed nest, people milled about on the deck high above us. For hours, our small boat circled the ship in the stormy sea. Everyone was seasick, vomiting over the railing. When dusk fell, the fire was still out of control, and with this final opportunity of escape eluding us, we headed back to land.

But my mother's guardian angel was watching over us. Or so she would have me believe. "Neither curse your fate, Totsu, nor wish for what you can never have," she advised.

The ships crossing the Baltic Sea during the German withdrawal were in constant danger of being bombed or torpedoed. The purposeful sinking of the *Wilhelm Gustoff*, which left from Poland after the collapse of the Eastern Front, is still considered the worst maritime disaster of all time. An estimated eight thousand people drowned in that tragedy. The convoy of troopships leaving Tallinn we were to join also received heavy Soviet bombardment. One of these ships, the *Moero* was filled to capacity with wounded soldiers and Estonian refugees. Over six hundred people were lost when it went down.

For us, however, the sun rose the next morning upon serene and sparkling waters. The fire continued burning, but had been brought under control and was confined inside the hold. We were able to embark, and, because it was late in leaving, our ship made the crossing peacefully and alone, the Russians unaware of its passage.

Standing on deck and singing the Estonian National Anthem, we watched the coastline recede. Many people brought along a handful of native soil, certain they would never see their homeland or loved ones again. For me, being on a big ship was a great new adventure. There were lots of soldiers in uniform. I kept my eyes open for my father, but didn't see anyone who resembled him. Already, the farm and Memme and even Rosencrantz Avenue seemed like a time and place from long ago.

Children ran around freely on deck. The adults, weepy and nostalgic, were indulgent of our innocent and joyful play. Marika Tamm was almost my age, and her little brother Enn was three. We played tag and hide-and-go-seek. Concealed under a bench, I found a lady's leather pocketbook. Ema and I took it to a ship's officer.

"*Gut, gut,*" he said, patting my head. "*Gute kleines Mädchen.*" I didn't understand, but my mother, like most other educated Estonians, not only spoke German, but also Russian, and had even studied English throughout all her years in school.

"He said you're a good little girl, Totsu," she told me, lifting me up to hug me tightly until I squirmed away.

The following morning the red roofs of Germany appeared in the golden dawn. The dangerous crossing was over. After we disembarked, it became obvious that we were now refugees. The soldiers went one way; the rest of us were herded into a large, noisy room to be numbered and tagged with our names and places of origin. The men were separated from the women and children. Crowded together, we were hauled in military transport trucks to a large detention centre consisting of abandoned army barracks, and assigned to our quarters.

The rooms were all the same—two rows of six bunk beds, each covered by a striped mattress. Ema and I slept on the bed assigned to us. The filthy mattress was crawling with bedbugs and lice and spotted with the blood of previous occupants. In the morning, the refugees gathered in the great muddy square to wash in long troughs. The bathrooms were ditches dug into the ground with a long pole to sit on. We were handed tin containers and spoons and stood in line for soup.

Fortunately, we didn't have to stay there for more than a few days. Director Liiva had connections. The architectural firm, in fact, was a German subsidiary. They took care of Hr. Liiva, and he took care of us.

5.
Dresden

THE NAME OF THE CITY itself may bring a twinge of horror to those who still recall the destruction. Although it was not on the scale of Hiroshima or Nagasaki, for the atom bomb had yet to be used, it was startling even within the normal atrocities of war.

In 1944, however, when the Director, Härra Liiva, was able to situate us there, it was the safest and most beautiful city in Germany. Having no major industries and thus escaping bombardment, it bore an enormous influx of people. In addition to wounded soldiers and prisoners of war, it accommodated approximately 200,000 refugees.

Ema and I were lodged in the sedate, well-kept house of an elderly German couple in the outskirts. Hr. Liiva's fortune supported us. Every day we took the tram to the centre of the city to see the sights and to visit the others: Hr. Liiva's family; Hr. Leps and his beautiful dark-haired bride; the Rauds, who were shortly expecting the birth of their baby; but mostly August Tamm, his wife, and their two children, Marika and Enn. There were also other Estonians in Dresden who had immigrated to Germany before the first Russian occupation in 1940. Often we stopped by at the Kotts, where Proua Kott, her grey hair knotted up in a bun and her round wrinkled face smiling like the moon, would always make a fuss over me. *Eat, eat child so you'll grow*, she would urge in a wavering voice, serving tiny sweetcakes from a flowered platter.

Ema and I spent every day together. When the weather was fine, we walked in the well-kept park by the river. People said that if the city was ever bombed, a large tract of woodland such as that would be even safer than the cellars. Often we would stop at the park zoo to look at the tigers, giraffes, bears, big snakes, and funny monkeys. Afterward we would meet other Estonians in a crowded restaurant in the centre of the city to eat *Gemüsesuppe* and sip sweet foamy dark beer from large glass steins. Along with the Tamm children, I went to the circus to see clowns, trapeze artists, trained lions, elephants doing tricks, and big white horses galloping around the rink with beautiful ladies in sequined outfits standing on their backs. We also saw a show in a puppet theatre where miniature poodles performed, wearing bonnets and dresses or suits and ties. They strutted upright on their tiny hind legs pushing baby carriages and even waltzed together. I wanted a dog of my own more than anything, but Ema said no.

It was my good fortune to possess one of those round rosy faces that always drew smiles from strangers. Children aren't impressed by charm, but grown-ups adored me. With my blonde hair, big blue eyes, and dimples, I remained a favourite of strangers on trams and of waitresses in restaurants. Even in this foreign city, the clerk in the sweetshop sometimes gave me a piece of candy. One day two *hausfraus* stopped on the sidewalk to admire me, speaking to my mother in German. To make her proud, I lifted my arm the way many grown-ups did when they happened to meet each other on the street and shouted *Heil Hitler!* The women were delighted. Ema smiled in return, but I felt her grip stiffen on my arm and I could tell something was wrong. Holding my hand tightly, she walked so fast toward home that I had to run to keep up. She didn't say a word until she closed the door behind us. Only then did I feel the full force of her rage.

"Don't you ever say that again, Tita," she whispered into my startled face, shaking me in rhythm with her words. "Do you understand? That's bad, bad, bad."

I never did.

In time, I came to understand.

Somehow my father managed to find us, as people did even during the greatest upheavals. The last time I had seen him was when he lifted me out of the motorcycle sidecar at 12 Rosencrantz Avenue in Tallinn. That seemed like a long, long time ago, though only a few months had elapsed.

Isa brought me a gift, a book inscribed in purple ink in his beautiful and precise handwriting: *To my dearest daughter, with the most heartfelt congratulations in honour of her sixth birthday.* It tells the story of a beautiful princess who is about to be sacrificed to the evil King of the Night and how she is finally saved by a poor fisherman's son. He wrote it on an old typewriter, sitting outside a tent in an army encampment, or so he said. It is the only memento I still possess from my early childhood. The pasteboard cover is torn and filthy from hundreds of readings, but the inside is well preserved, painstakingly typed in columns of red and black ink and beautifully illustrated with small drawings and larger renderings in watercolour.

Since he was still in the military, the visit was brief. Ema told him about our escape from Tallinn and explained why we couldn't get to Sweden as planned. Isa showed us the shrapnel wounds in his legs and told us that he had been unconscious for some time from a hard blow on the head, alive only because he was wearing his steel helmet. "Crippled in the legs and addled in the brain," he joked, but he did not find it funny when I repeated this later in front of other people.

He had been in Hamburg when it was bombed. In a railroad station in Berlin, he had seen well-dressed Jews displaying six-pointed stars prodded into cattle cars with pitchforks by Nazi commandoes.

No! my mother exclaimed.

"It's true," he said. "There are more horrors in this world than you could ever imagine, dear Emps."

She didn't believe him, I could tell. My father was known to exaggerate.

All the major cities were receiving heavy bombardment, he told her. America had joined the war. He was certain that Germany would be defeated. This did not displease him. He hated the Nazis almost as much as the Communists.

"But what will happen to us then?" Ema asked.

There was no answer.

Later, their conversation became more personal.

All night they fought, hissing words to each other as they lay together in the narrow bed on the other side of the room. The words would get louder, until they were shouting.

"You are my wife. You owe it to me."

"I owe you nothing."

"It's that damned Nazi, Gusti Tamm, isn't it?"

"What have you ever done for us? All you ever cared about was yourself."

"Stop. Stop it!" I cried, waking up, pressing my hands over my ears. "Please, please, please stop."

But they couldn't stop.

I didn't understand the full meaning of the words they were shouting at each other, but what I did perceive was the oppressive, thick stench of disappointment and jealousy and frustration and rage.

Onu Gusti often came to see my mother, but sometimes we went to visit his family so I could play with Marika and Enn.

We would lay out our wooden building sets to make a city. Enn was a pest, pretending to be an airplane and bombing our constructions. One time Marika and I got into an argument. She called her large block with the tower a church, whereas I, being older, knew very well it was a cathedral. Marika went to play with her brother instead.

It was then I made the mistake of going into the grown-up room. The women—Proua Liiva, the beautiful, long-haired Pr. Leps with her red lips and fingernails, Pr. Raud with the baby in her belly, Onu Gusti's wife, and my mother—were drinking coffee and smoking cigarettes. No one paid any attention to me. I tried to crawl into my mother's lap. She told me to shush and shooed me aside, but I needed attention and refused to shush.

"Where's Onu Gusti?" I whined loudly to my mother.

"Shush, Tita," she whispered, pinching my arm, hard.

"Ouch!" I yelped, pulling away from her nasty grip.

The women were smiling at me, and I felt safe and warm in the circle of their approbation.

"Do you like Onu Gusti?" the Director's wife asked, humouring me.

"He comes to visit us all the time," I said.

The room became silent then.

"Why does he visit you?" Pr. Liiva encouraged, leaning forward in a friendly manner.

I always did like to perform and I could feel all their eyes focused upon me. "Because he is in love with Ema."

"And how do you know that?" she asked.

"They hug a lot."

The women were waiting for more.

"They kiss a lot too."

Still they waited.

"Then they send me out to play, so I can't tell you any more."

It was over.

I curtsied then, at my cutest.

My audience laughed and clapped and I was pleased with my performance, until I turned around to see my mother's bruised face. She pretended to be laughing with the rest but I knew I had betrayed her. We never did visit Onu Gusti's family again, although he still came to see us often.

One time he took my mother to a movie theatre and she insisted that I come along. He said it wasn't a good idea and she should leave the child with the German couple. And he was right. Children under twelve were *Verbotten*. Ema tried to convince the man in the ticket booth that I was very well-behaved and would sit quietly in her lap, but I believe it was my big blue eyes that finally won him over.

What we saw wasn't like a normal theatre at all where actors performed on a stage. People were huge; sometimes you only saw their enormous faces. Although I didn't understand the words, I can still remember the beautiful blonde woman, the star, who wore a silver fur coat and sang. She was stuck on a passenger train stalled by an avalanche in the Austrian Alps. A handsome young peasant, who was really a prince in disguise, fell in love with her. Before the film ended, I had to pee very badly and was wiggling so much in Ema's lap that we had to leave, saying *Bitte, bitte* as we crawled over a long row of grown-up knees. The WC was in the outer lobby. Once you left the theatre, you couldn't get back in again unless you bought another ticket.

"I told you we shouldn't have brought her," Onu Gusti complained.

Ema didn't say anything, but I could tell she was disappointed. She would have been angrier still if I had wet my pants in the theatre while sitting on her lap.

To commemorate my sixth birthday, Ema took me to have my picture taken. In the photograph, I am wearing the blue-and-pink striped angora sweater she knit for me, my hair fluffed out properly the way she liked it, but my eyes are large with fear and my lips are undecided, for just as the shot was about to be taken, the air raid siren sounded. At the same time, from behind the black cloth, the photographer raised his arm to display a funny little yellow bird. It didn't produce the smile he wanted but it averted the tears, so he decided to take a chance on the picture. The resulting image depicts the exact moment on a child's countenance between tears and laughter, a significant encapsulation of my life.

The ALL CLEAR sounded a few moments later.

Even though Dresden had never been bombed, it served to remind us that the world is always at war and that no one is ever safe.

6.
February, 1945

WITHOUT HIS KNOWLEDGE, my father left me an unappreciated legacy. In my twenties, the veins in my left leg began to swell, fortunately on the inner side of the knee so it didn't show too much. Varicose veins. Over the years, the condition worsened. It became unsightly but also dangerous, for the blood could pool at the ankles and become very painful. Something had to be done. Rather than go to the hospital to have the veins stripped, I opted for endovenous laser treatment, which, though expensive, would take only a few hours.

Everything was progressing well. The only part of the procedure that some patients minded—the freezing of the veins—was over. We were discussing literature, the doctor and I, trying to assess whether any current male authors were truly able to capture the viewpoint of a woman, an amusing and absorbing conversation. I was totally relaxed. We both put on protective eyewear as he prepared to use the laser upon the weakened veins. "You may notice a peculiar odour and experience a strange taste in the back of your throat," he warned.

At the smell of burning flesh, I felt a constriction in my chest which became stronger until the pain was almost unbearable. "There's this immense pressure in my chest," I managed, trying to remain calm.

"Relax," he attempted to reassure me, "this is the easy part. We're nearly done," though it was quite apparent that he too was concerned as I experienced what seemed like a genuine and quite unexpected panic attack, panting and covered in a cold sweat.

I took some deep breaths as he checked my heart and helped

me out of the reclining chair. After the procedure, patients are required to walk around for thirty minutes to enhance blood circulation in the legs. Although the pain in my chest gradually subsided, I still felt weak and shaken. He checked my heart again. Everything appeared to be normal. "Does this happen often?" I asked.

The doctor shook his head. "I've performed hundreds of these treatments for more than ten years," he said. "It's never happened before. I can't explain it." After a while, however, I thought I could. The recollection of a particular smell outlasts conscious memory. My senses recalled and my body reacted.

In the past, it was believed by Christians and Jews alike that God caused the disasters that befell humanity. In Noah's time and after, He wiped out whole populations, according to the Bible, for not respecting His will or His laws. Even now, we are occasionally reminded of a Godly wrath not of our own making—a tornado, a hurricane, an earthquake, a tsunami. But man has taken the greater part of mass destruction upon himself, regularly killing his own kind in incomprehensible numbers.

Sixty-two million, five hundred thirty-seven thousand, six hundred has been established as the total death count for World War II. Most historians conveniently round this off to 62.5 million. *Thirty-seven thousand six-hundred* lives are thus twice eliminated.

Thirty-seven million soldiers (rounded off) were sacrificed in World War I (not counting the civilians). Between *two million and two million five hundred thousand* Southeast Asian lives were taken in Vietnam (not counting the military).

I feel deep sorrow for a mother who loses her baby to illness, for a child whose parents die in an automobile accident, for the old folks who remain to grieve for their family killed in a plane crash. These are tragedies and horrors that many have to endure in life. We all must die. But how can one comprehend the purposeful murder of millions? A million (1,000,000) only takes up seven spaces, less than an inch, no matter which way you write it. Line up the corpses and then measure the distance. Sympathy becomes irrelevant. Anger is insufficient. One can only feel a deep and abiding sense of revulsion and disbelief.

It is indeed possible that more humans are killed by other humans than the total of those who have lived out their natural life span: murdered, maimed, tortured, their livelihood and offspring destroyed, their natural world decimated. For what reason? To enhance the affluence of the victorious? To satisfy the ego of a dictator? To increase the glory of some particular god? THE SPECIES THAT ANNIHILATED ITSELF—shall this serve as our epitaph?

When the air raid sounds it is often merely a warning: ENEMY PLANES APPROACHING. All normal activity stops. You raise your head to listen. There is nothing overhead but unfathomable endless space. Soon the sirens sound again: ALL CLEAR. You can cook a meal, visit a museum, attend school, plant seeds in the tilled ground and hope for a harvest. You have not been selected as a target this time. You can go on living.

If the siren is followed by the discernible roar of approaching aircraft however, you quickly head for shelter. Unlike the strong wind of a tornado or a hurricane which wreaks havoc above but leaves underground burrows undisturbed, bombs can destroy you wherever you hide, your former existence signified only by the abhorrent stink of your decaying corpse. You sit quietly in the cellar nevertheless, trying to be brave, hoping that this time luck is with you. Like a rabbit you cower, hearing the wings of the hawk as it dives for its prey. The hunter has learned the trick from nature—he whistles lightly through his lips to imitate the sound of flight and the rabbit remains immobile, hunching down into the undergrowth. That is what the hunter counts upon as he aims his rifle and shoots.

What you do with this brief time as you wait for death is up to you. In Tallinn, Memme prayed, and I huddled in her lap crying until I fell asleep. *That's only the anti-aircraft, Totsu,* my mother would say to comfort me, *they're defending us and shooting down the planes.* But there was no mistaking the sound of the bombs as they fell from the sky, the hiss of their imminent arrival. If you heard the explosion, you knew you had been spared until the next one.

Dresden had no defence, for it was never regarded as a target but as a place of long-established culture and filled with civilians. There were no military installations, no factories producing weapons for warfare. This was a mission of revenge based on a different strategy—to destroy morale. On the evening of February 13, 1945, the sirens that sounded in Dresden were not followed by the ALL CLEAR, but by the thunder of planes overhead. The explosions we heard were the detonations of bombs hitting their mark.

Seven hundred and ninety-six British aircraft released one thousand four hundred seventy-eight tons of high explosives. And shortly thereafter, one thousand one hundred eighty-two tons of incendiary bombs (later perfected into napalm). The explosives blew off the roofs of buildings to expose the timbers, thus allowing the bombs to ignite them easily and create a self-sustaining firestorm of fifteen hundred degrees Centigrade. For those in the centre of the city, there was nowhere to hide.

The basement of the German household in which we lived on the outskirts of Dresden was not like our dark cellar in Tallinn. It was furnished with tables and chairs and a sofa. There was a storeroom filled with toys left over from children who had grown up and gone away. While Ema and the old German couple played cards to pass the time, I was allowed to explore among the toys. I found a doll and a beautiful baby carriage to put her in, wheeling her around to soothe her as the house shook and outside was bright daylight in the middle of the night. We ignored it all. We were brave. We pretended everything was normal.

ALL CLEAR sounded then, and we thought it was over. But the strategy was to hamper the efforts of the fire services and rescue units, so three hours later the sirens warned of another attack: Five hundred twenty-nine British planes dropped one thousand eight hundred tons of bombs to finish things off.

Even that was not deemed sufficient, for in the morning they came again: Three hundred eleven American B-17s dropped seven hundred seventy-one tons of bombs, just to make sure.

Some other numbers impossible for me to comprehend:

In one night, three thousand nine hundred tons of bombs were dropped on Dresden and two hundred fifty thousand, or one hundred thousand, or thirty-five thousand, or twenty-five thousand civilians were annihilated. (The estimates vary, for who really knows.)

Fifteen square kilometres of the inner city were decimated.

Memories are not only photographs of what you experience, but also what you saw that you were never meant to see, what you heard that you were not supposed to hear, what you felt, touched, smelled, and forgot.

After it was over, I was never allowed to see the destruction of the inner city, and Ema refused to look. We stayed away. But some went to bear witness. And talked about what they had seen. And I listened because I was not supposed to hear.

What used to be streets and avenues were impassable with the refuse of corpses lying untended.

Charred human skeletons clutched each other on the iron benches of the disintegrated park which was safe from bombs but not from the firestorm that followed.

Burnt animals in steel cages.

People broiled alive in shelters.

The children, the wounded, the old, the young yearning for life, those yet unborn, the animals, the trees, the irreplaceable artefacts of civilization preserved for centuries, tokens of affection, the heights of creation and aspiration, hope, and glory, gone, wiped out forever. The little dogs performing in their human outfits in the theatre. The elephants in the circus. The funny apes we watched at the zoo. The ducks we fed in the lake. Hr. Leps and his beautiful dark-haired wife with her red lips and fingernails. The Rauds waiting for their baby. Hr. and Pr. Kott who served us tea and cakes and made us welcome in their home. Gone. All gone. Part of the nameless horde. Refugees seeking shelter, never counted in the registered total presumed to have died on this night.

I didn't see it, but I remembered.

I heard, though I was not supposed to listen.

I breathed in the stench of the burnt flesh and forgot.

Some people survived. Like us, they happened to be living in the outer regions of the city: Director Liiva and his family; Onu Gusti, his wife, and his children; a few other Estonians we had met when we arrived. Human beings are resilient. Adaptable. Those lucky enough to escape death live on.

Dresden also has been restored. If it were not for the persistence of recorded memory, no one would now suspect that anything horrible ever took place there. In spring, new grass sprouts from the land and dandelions grow from the cracks in the sidewalk. The rubble is cleared away and eventually a new city emerges from the desecration of the old. This particular scar on the collective face of humanity gradually fades. It is barely remembered now, replaced by other wars and more recent atrocities.

In order to exist, the military mind must banish compassion, for how can a soldier look upon the enemy as a human being like himself and still follow orders? So we battle redskins, niggers, micks, wops, kikes, krauts, chinks, nips, commies, gooks, pakis, ragheads, terrorists, insurgents—for it is impossible to maintain humanitarian sensibilities in a war. *Those people are used to death. They don't feel grief like we do. Kill the bastards.* And after the war is over? Is it still possible to live a semblance of a normal life without repressing memory?

Ema and I left Dresden shortly after. Onu Gusti came with us. I didn't ask about his family. Why wasn't he with Marika and Enn and their mother? I was six years old. I had learned that it was better to keep my mouth shut and my wonderings to myself. We went by train, traveling south to Austria to once again escape the communist advance. It was not like the train I saw in the movie, full of red velvet seats and richly dressed passengers. We sat on our suitcases in a cattle car watching from the open doorway as we passed through the devoured landscape of Germany until I fell asleep in my mother's arms. I dreamed of war.

The sky was filled with planes. I woke up crying.

The mind recalls events and emotions. The body records.

When I went to have my legs checked six weeks after the laser treatment, I mentioned to the doctor what I thought may have been the cause of my panic attack.

"It's very possible," he said.

7.
Ehrwald

IN THE VILLAGE OF EHRWALD at the foot of the Zugspits, the highest of the Austrian Alps, everything was white: The craggy peaks, the foothills, the broad meadows, the roofs of houses, and the feather mattress on my bed, puffed up so high that I had to climb the steps of a small footstool in order to sink down into the snowy softness which soon became cozy and warm.

We were in the White Country. The Russians were red, the French green, the Finnish yellow, the Swedes purple, the English pink. Americans and Canadians from beyond the great ocean still remained grey and unsubstantial to me, like shadows. Estonians were blue, black, and white, like the flag. Blue for the sky, black for the earth, and white for our pure hearts. That's what it said in the song Ema taught me, the Estonian National Anthem. All three verses. I already knew the Lord's Prayer. Memme taught me that.

Ema claimed that when summer comes and everything turns green again, the peaks of the Zugspits remain covered in snow. I didn't believe her. Even I could see that the tops of mountains were much closer to the sun.

"Mothers are always right, Totsu," she said.

We lived on the second floor of a wooden house. The old Austrian woman who was the owner lived downstairs. We kept to ourselves, and no one came to visit. We listened to the radio. We played cards. We sang songs.

Even though it was winter, I spent a lot of time outside. Ema built a playhouse for me in a high snow bank, stomping around with her big boots to make a circle. Inside this she moulded a large round table, spending a lot of time smoothing the top and sides with her mittened hands to make it look perfect. Then she carved out four chairs with high backs and comfortable seats, large enough for even her to sit on. I made snowball people and served them snow cakes and ice tea. Sometimes Ema came too and we would have a party. In my snow house I had my mother to myself.

I never liked Onu Gusti. I hated his thinning, slicked-back hair, his shiny porous nose, his snake-lipped smirk above the brown striped gabardine of his worn-out suit. He wasn't nearly as handsome as my father in his uniform. Why didn't he go back to his family where he belonged? He had children of his own, Marika and Enn. Where were they now? I was afraid to ask.

Onu Gusti didn't like me either. I could tell, although he pretended otherwise.

And how is the little one today? he would offer, reaching down to ruffle my hair, which always made me cringe.

Even now I recall with distaste his manner of pausing between small groupings of words to swallow spittle, which caused his enormous Adam's apple to march up and down his skinny neck, and his hissy laughter as he forced the air between his teeth. My impression might be quite different if we met as adults, but the memory is all I have.

Ema hardly paid attention to me when he was around, which was most of the time. I chewed my nails and watched them. Once when we were alone in my snow house, I asked about Isa.

"Your father is in a hospital not too far away," she told me.

How they kept in contact, I never knew, but my father always seemed aware of our whereabouts.

"Oh no," she continued, seeing my stricken face, "he wasn't wounded in the war. He's just being treated for stomach ulcers."

It sounded like an insult the way she said it. Was I alert enough at six to perceive that? I think so. But then again, everything becomes seasoned with the patina of memory.

"Maybe we'll go visit him. Would you like that?"

And we did go. By bus? By car? On the train? I don't recall. I do remember that during this trip Ema reminded me several times not to call my father *Onu* by mistake.

I was eager to see Isa again, but also apprehensive. Would they fight like they did in Dresden the last time we were together? I had to keep my fingers in my ears then to shut out the mean words. At the hospital, however, I found my fears groundless. No children under twelve were allowed inside. *Halt! Verbotten.* This time my mother didn't coax or argue.

In Erhwald we were safe from bombings. There weren't enough people in this village to kill. Only women, children, and the elderly remained. Sometimes we did hear a dim rumble overhead, but it was only snow sliding down the steep sides of mountains.

"Avalanches," Ema explained. "The snow softens in the spring and falls off the peaks."

"Like in the movie," I shouted, remembering.

"Like an enormous snowball," Onu Gusti added. "If it becomes big enough, it can bury an entire village. Sometimes enemy planes drop bombs on purpose just to make this happen."

"Don't scare the child, Gusti. Can't you see she's frightened of everything already?"

But he merely confirmed what I had already determined in my heart—no place in the world is ever safe.

Ema worried that I was spending too much time alone. They discussed me, unaware that I was always listening.

Onu Gusti suggested they enrol me in a German kindergarten. "She's six. Surely she's old enough," he said. "It'll be good for her to spend some time with other children. She'll learn the language."

I didn't want to go. In Tallinn, I was taken to kindergarten when I was three, the youngest in the class. The older kids teased me, calling me a *beebi*. Karin, who was five, would often pinch me hard on the arm whenever the teacher wasn't looking. I sneaked a candy from home to make her like me.

"You better bring me another one," she demanded, unwrapping it slowly and popping it into her mouth. "If you don't, I'll beat you up."

The following morning, Memme caught my hand in the candy jar.

"I know you're lying," Karin said, "but I'll give you another chance. Here. Take this teensy-weensy bit of paper. If you don't bring it back to me tomorrow, you'll be sorry."

Of course, I lost it, but I didn't recall any retribution. Perhaps the war intervened, or my illness, and I didn't have to go to kindergarten any more.

In Erwhald, I begged Ema to please not make me go, but it had already been decided. Dressed in my best skirt and sweater, my hair combed, and a *tutt* fixed in my hair, she took me by the hand down the snow-covered road to the schoolhouse.

I was no longer the youngest. The trouble was, I couldn't speak the language. In addition to the forbidden *Heil Hitler*, I also knew:

Ja woll, Nein;
Danke schön, Bitte;
Guten Nacht, auf Wiedersehen;
Verbotten! Halt!

And I could count from one to ten.

They were not aware that I was able to read when I was three, that I could count to a hundred, that I had once performed alone on stage wearing a red velvet dress with a lace collar, that I knew the difference between a church and a cathedral and that my father was a brave soldier who fought for his country. When I entered the classroom, I had no idea how to be like them. I never sat behind a desk in a straight row, nor marched in a straight line, nor regulated my bladder to the hours of the clock. When we lined up to go to the bathroom, I washed my hands like the other children, but had no need to use the toilet. I was well-disciplined, but not yet regimented.

Later, sitting in class in our assigned places, I raised my hand for the teacher's attention.

Bitte? I asked, wiggling my bottom and crossing my legs, trying to communicate my need.

She frowned her skinny brows, but then relented. *Ja woll*, she said, pointing at the door.

Danke schön, I curtsied, hurrying down the hallway, searching for the proper place.

So many doors all the same. I didn't know what to do except

to go outside, squatting in a snow bank like an animal, hoping no one saw me, leaving a bright yellow spot as a mark of my disgrace. I was grateful that I had been taught to always memorize my address wherever we happened to be or I never would have found my way back to *1A—Kindergarten.*

Twenty faces looked up at me as I entered. None were smiling.

Afraid of getting lost again, I spent noon recess waiting by the door until we were herded back in. We were then each given a mat and a designated space on the floor. For a whole hour, we had to lie quietly on our mats, resting.

Bitte? I asked once again.

The tall white shadow above me pointed a stern finger to my mat. *Nein*, she said through stiff firm lips.

I squirmed, trying to hold on with all my might, but the wet warmth spread out silently beneath me. When the teacher finally clapped her hands, all the children stood up and folded their mats. Everyone except me. I remained on the floor trying to cover up the stain.

Auslander, someone whispered loudly. *Dumkoff!* There was a great deal of tittering and pointing, until the teacher put a stop to it.

I wept that night into the softness of my feather bed. Something must be wrong with me. I was six years old and still wetting my pants!

"I don't want to go," I begged my mother, "please don't make me go."

The next morning, despite all my whining and pleading, she took me firmly by the hand once again and marched me back to school. The teacher motioned her into a room to talk privately.

"Tell her there's something wrong with me. Tell her to explain to the class that I can't help it. That I was damaged in the war."

They left me waiting by the door—red-faced and miserable, a *Dumkoff Auslander.*

When they finally emerged, it was obvious that things had been settled. These people did not want me in their school. Without giving me a glance, the teacher hurried down the hall to her classroom. My mother and I walked slowly back home. Though she didn't say anything at all, I felt her disappointment by the hard way she held my hand and there was no way I could make her feel any better.

8.
Invasion

IT WAS LATE SPRING, not yet summer. Hausfraus scrubbed steps and sidewalks with stiff brushes dipped in soapy water. Onu Gusti, Ema, and I spent whole days hiking through the Alpine meadows. I picked bouquets for my mother, and she wove flowers into crowns for me. After we ate the sandwiches she brought, I was allowed to take off my shoes and socks to dabble my feet in the cold waters of the mountain streams. The high peaks of the Zugspits remained white with snow like Ema said they would.

"It's only a matter of time now," Onu Gusti predicted, gazing off into the distance.

One morning there was an announcement on the radio.

The *Führer* was dead. *Heil Hitler* was done for. The war was over. Allied troops would soon be marching into Austria.

For us, this was the beginning of something yet to be determined. For the woman whose home we lived in, and for the rest of the villagers, the invasion had a much greater significance. Everything they looked upon as their own would no longer belong to them. The enemy won the war. A foreign power would enforce new rules. Their world will never be the same.

Onu Gusti attempted to reassure our landlady that in Erwhald the invasion would most likely be peaceful. As there was no resistance, there was no need to worry. Nevertheless, with shaking hands she hung a white sheet from a second-storey window as a symbol of surrender. The other houses up and down the street were similarly festooned.

"There's no one left here to fight," Onu Gusti reiterated, "I'm sure there won't be any trouble. But then again...."

Who was coming? I wondered. The Russians who bombed Tallinn? Or the British who bombed Dresden? Or maybe the Americans who bombed the mountain peaks to cause avalanches? For once I was brave enough to ask, but still too young to understand. Many years later I find that I will never be old enough to comprehend the rationalizations regarding any war.

Ema packed a bag with extra food, warm clothing, and blankets, and very early the next morning we hiked further into the mountains than we had ever gone before. Through the meadows, up the foothills, into the high forest. In the evening Onu Gusti cut some limbs to build a lean-to, while Ema gathered up smaller boughs to cushion the ground where we would sleep. My job was to collect dry sticks for firewood so we could heat soup for our supper. Although we heard a few distant explosions during the day and an occasional zing of bullets, there was no sustained artillery fire. The night remained quiet, the sky a black canopy filled with innumerable stars. I counted as many as I could before I fell asleep.

The next day, when we walked back down the hillside, there was no one about. The village was silent. Everyone remained inside. We went to our room to wait along with the others. Late in the afternoon we heard something—the sound of hundreds of tramping feet coming closer. I ran to the window. Columns of soldiers in green uniforms holding rifles on their shoulders passed by down below, their black boots clacking in unison on the pavement. Between the marching squadrons were jeeps and trucks. A few tanks rolled by, taking up the whole width of the street. The soldiers seemed in good spirits, talking and laughing, not the kind of men who would kill people. One of them looked up and gave me a small salute, his hand lifting to the peak of his cap. I leaned out as far as I dared to wave back. He smiled and blew me a kiss.

I was filled with happiness. *The war is over. There is nothing more to worry about.*

It was then I felt a sharp pinch on my backside and squealed loudly in surprise. "I told you to get away from there," Ema scolded, pulling me from the window and giving me several hard shakes. "You have to obey your mother, Tita, when you're asked to do something," she added, taking me by the ear to stand in the corner facing the wall.

"I never heard you," I whined, but had to remain there in impotent rage until the parade was over, pouting at the injustices so common to every childhood.

"It's not at all seemly, Totsu, to wave at the conquering troops marching into the village while we're living in a German household," she tried to explain to me later.

Why not? I wondered. *Isn't everyone happy that the war is over?*

"I don't understand," I replied, crying real tears now. "I didn't mean to be bad."

Even to this day, my unsophisticated brain does not comprehend. If everyone truly wants peace, why are there wars? When human beings murder their own kind, where is the victory?

You have to fight for what you believe, Ema says.
I believe in not fighting.
You are always so negative.
True.

Negative spaces have captured my attention ever since I was a child: black footprints in a field of newly fallen snow; not *what* people believe, but why they do; not the action, but what motivates it; not the victory of war, but the resulting loss.

For you, Ema, foreground is important: the phantasmagoria of the red petals of the peony.

For me: The pattern of its shadow upon the wall.

You like to be in front, leading the troops, waving the flag and patriotically singing the national anthem.

I prefer to stay in the background, negating the flow of platitudes.

We are, of course, conversing in the confined space of a single consciousness—my own.

For a short while after the occupation, our life in Ehrwald remained much the same. We continued our daily walks in the mountains, one time coming upon an abandoned Allied military encampment, a glorious moment, an unexpected find of hidden treasure. For hours we foraged, discovering a few rusty unopened tins of Spam and of beans, the stub of a pencil, crumpled wads of paper with words written in English, half-smoked cigarettes. I spent the rest of the time searching for butts, tearing off the paper and saving the tobacco in a tin can which I planned to keep as a present for my father should I ever see him again.

Scratching around in the dirt, Ema discovered the husk of a hard red candy, sucked on and discarded. That night she unwrapped the morsel from her handkerchief and washed off the dirt.

"Here, Totsu," she said.

I can still see the look on her face as she placed the candy into my waiting mouth.

We left Ehrwald shortly after. Despite truly enormous challenges, it didn't take long for the Allied bureaucracy to spring into action. Now that the killing and destroying were over, reconstruction and rehabilitation could begin. The United Nations Refugee Relief Association (UNRRA) went to work cleaning up the flotsam and jetsam of the millions of people floating aimlessly around the German wreckage. Food stamps were issued to those with proof of German citizenship. The rest were herded together into hundreds of camps set up throughout Germany and Austria, administered mostly by Americans. Military barracks, vacant youth camps, apartment complexes, confiscated private homes, even abandoned castles were filled to capacity with refugees. An incredible number of displaced people had to be housed and fed and clothed after they were rounded up and accounted for. It was a successful intervention. Newsreels displayed groups of smiling children, saved at last. Years later, while watching old documentaries about WWII, I thought perhaps I would see someone I knew or even myself, but I never have.

For the displaced, documents became the most important possessions in life. If you didn't have your papers, you were done for. There was no place for you in the system. The greatest fear was repatriation—being sent back to the land you fled from. Ema and I were assigned to a DP camp in Landeck, Austria, not so far from Ehrwald. Onu Gusti had to go elsewhere to be registered with his wife and his children, since they had entered Germany together, and I was very happy to have my mother to myself once again.

A life is truly perceived only in its entirety. From birth to death. The highs and lows are merely storms endured during the passage. Thus, although my emotional imprint of Onu Gusti remains unaltered, as an adult, I have to consider other possibilities. To be fair, I must acknowledge that without him, my mother and I may not have survived at all. He was a man like any other, perhaps better than most. Certainly, he must have been talented and ambitious, for in 1968, at the Museum of Modern Art in New York City, I came across his name once again—August Tamm. In an exhibition devoted to modern architecture, his designs were prominently displayed.

"I can't believe it!" I gasped out loud to my husband. "That's Onu Gusti!"

I had heard long before that Gusti and his family had immigrated to New York, but by then his odious presence had faded from my consciousness. When I mentioned the display to my mother, she didn't seem the least bit surprised. Yes, she informed me, he had resumed his architectural career and had become a very successful man. But she offered nothing else, and, to protect us both, I never asked.

9.
Landeck

ONCE LABELLED, YOU ARE seen as something you never were before. We had now become DPs. Depending on circumstances, the appellation provoked sympathy or dismissal, but always in a tone of belittlement.

Nestled within an equally picturesque Alpine Valley, our new home in Landeck consisted of rows of barracks surrounded by barbed wire, not to keep us in but to keep others out. Here all our basic needs were met. We were given food and water, a place to wash and to defecate, and a bed to sleep in. The camp administrators lived in confiscated private houses at the entrance to the compound, one of which was converted into offices.

My mother and I were assigned to Room B in Barrack 31 and issued two packets of clean bedding. I got to carry them as Ema had her hands full with our suitcases. The room was small, containing three single beds, each with a narrow metal wardrobe. Two of the beds were covered with clean mattresses. Upon the third, already made up, sat an older girl, almost a woman. To me she looked like a beautiful fairy princess. Backlit from the window by the late afternoon sun, her long curly hair shone like gold. She was perched on the very edge of the bed, her feet weighted to the floor by heavy laced-up leather shoes.

"Tere?" she said in a timid voice, raising only her eyes, as if asking permission to greet us.

She was Estonian!

"Tere! Tere!" my mother cried out, setting down the suitcases to extend her arms.

The girl stood up, and they clung to each other like long lost friends or family. We spoke the same language. We bore the same losses. We knew things about each other that were impossible to reveal to someone from another place or time.

Her name was Virve and she seemed like a grown-up to me, although she couldn't have been more than sixteen. She was all alone in the world, she told my mother. At night when I pretended to be asleep, they talked. Ema had the middle bed and they spoke softly. I had to lift my head from the pillow so I could listen with both ears.

"I have nobody," Virve said. "I have nothing. I don't know whether my family is alive or dead."

When the Russian troops occupied her village, she escaped only because she had an after-school job in a nearby town and the shopkeeper took her along in his truck when he fled with his wife and children. Like us, they were able to get passage on a troopship to Germany. Upon landing, she was taken into a large room for questioning.

"I had to stand in front of a table of German officers. One did the talking while the others watched. I understood some of what he said from my German in school. I gave my name, my age, where I was born, the names of my parents. He asked if I had any diseases, if I was sick. *Nein*, I said. He motioned me to take off my jacket, then my shoes and stockings. My sweater, my skirt. He told me to turn this way and that, to bend over and touch my toes. We have to make sure you are healthy, he said. I was embarrassed. Clumsy. It was hard for me to understand. The other men were laughing at me. Then he motioned about my undershirt and panties...."

I raised my head higher to hear better which turned out to be a mistake.

"Shhh," said Ema, glancing over at me. "Shhh, the child."

I never did hear the rest.

Soon we learned that there were other Estonians in the Landeck DP Camp. Perhaps forty or fifty. Many were young (though older than Virve) and single. Some were middle-aged and married. There were no old people. Like Memme, they were left behind.

Mostly they were placed together into two large rooms which

formerly held German soldiers. During the day, the men sat on the beds, smoking hand-rolled cigarettes that they called *paberossi*. They played cards using their suitcases as tables, while the women mended and sewed and knit. At night, they hung blankets on ropes between the beds for a degree of privacy. Several communal bathhouses were available for camp use, with rows of toilets and sinks where we could wash ourselves and our clothes in cold water. There was also a building containing a kitchen where everyone lined up twice a day for food.

People with young children were assigned the smaller rooms formerly occupied by officers. Next door to us lived an Estonian boy named Toomas with his parents. He was five, a year younger than me. Overpowered by shyness, I kept away from him, preferring to make up my own world, my own games.

Ema allowed me to play outside as long as I stayed within view of our window. Sheltered by the wall of the barrack, I built a farm. First, I cleared the land, marking it off with sticks broken into even sections to serve as fences. The farmhouse, the garden, the orchard, the barn with stalls for the cows and horses, the fields where they grazed, the pigsty, the coop for the hens and rooster—all had to be constructed. It was an immense undertaking. Memories of the farm where I stayed with Memme came back to me, though Ema and I never spoke about her or anything related to our past. I gathered spotted stones to serve as cows, larger darker ones for horses, small white ones for sheep, pinkish round pebbles for pigs, and little yellow and speckled ones for chickens. Fields had to be ploughed. Crops planted. Hay made to feed the livestock. Grain scattered for the birds. Scraps fed to the pigs. I was busy from dawn until dusk. Ema had to call me several times before I ceased my labour.

Then one morning everything was gone. Swept away. The house, the barn, my animals, my crops, the substantial amount of grass I had pulled out and piled into neat round piles to dry—all had disappeared. I ran inside, wailing.

"What's happened, Totsu?" Ema cried.

She stood up from her sewing, her eyes full of alarm. Quickly she checked me over to make sure there was no blood and nothing was broken.

"What hurts?" she asked.

"I do," I sobbbed. "My farm. They've destroyed it. It's gone."

Ema smiled then, relief flooding her face.

"It's just that the caretaker raked around the barracks. That's his job, to keep everything neat and tidy. You can start on another one and make it even better," she said, wiping my nose.

"No, I can't," I replied.

And I never did.

Is the hurt smaller when a person is little? It may be easier to forget when one is six, but the brain stores all experience for future reference.

I made friends with Toomas after that, and we ran around the camp together like puppies loosed from the chain, sniffing here and digging there. For the remaining weeks of summer, we were wild and free. Round-headed, round-eyed Toomas his short brown hair standing up in straight bristles, appeared chubby, but of course he wasn't. Everyone was thin in those times. His parents obviously adored him. One could tell by the way their eyes always followed his swift passage. They called him "Little Burr."

Like bees after nectar, moths at a light, ants gathering around spilled sugar, the DP children began to hover around the Americans. These invaders weren't here to plunder; they brought riches to the downtrodden: chocolates, cigarettes, nylon stockings, a promise of more where that came from. *Amis* we called them.

Often a group of them sat outside on sunny afternoons drinking beer or spirits, loud and jolly, and sometimes tossed something over the porch railing to watch the little DPs scramble. Toomas managed to grab a piece of chocolate, but, reluctant to assert myself, I never got anything. One soldier must have noticed this, for he threw something directly at me. Even the silver wrapping was beautiful, and I smoothed it out for safekeeping. But the candy was awful. Sweet at first, no matter how much I chewed, it remained in my mouth like a lump of gristle.

"Pah," I said to Toomas, opening my mouth to show him the sticky wad. "This is not good at all."

"Spit it out," he suggested. "We'll bury it and make a funeral."

I had been taught politeness. When something is put on your plate, you must eat it all. I chewed and chewed, but finally had to remove it from my mouth and break it into small enough bits to be swallowed. Later I learned that it was just meant to be chewed. DPs called it "cow gum."

Soon Aid Packages began to arrive. Boxes of used clothing were placed in the central area where we received our food ration. We were allowed take whatever we needed. Ema was always very clever at making new things out of old—unravelling sweaters into yarn to knit new ones; removing threadbare parts of fabric and cutting out patterns from the rest to make clothes for me. She sewed a dress for herself from an old pair of tweed pants, covering the moth-holes with little tufts of brown wool for a decorative effect and, since there wasn't quite enough material, fashioning the shoulders from small swatches of a matching brown. This was the dress she wore as her best during our remaining years in Europe. From a green army coat, she made a Bavarian dirndl skirt for me and embroidered it with Alpine flowers. My feet had grown a lot since we left Tallinn, so she cut away the toes and heels of my old shoes to turn them into sandals. I felt very grown-up wearing them. She knit hats, mittens, and stockings, and made me a warm coat for winter.

During daylight hours, we were permitted to leave the camp as long as we checked ourselves out with the guard on duty at the main gate. Sometimes at night, the men would sneak through the barbed wire in the back of the compound to steal vegetables from the farmers' fields. I was not supposed to know this, but I always tried to hear as much as I could.

One sunny morning, Ema suggested that we go hiking in the mountains like we used to in Ehrwald. Neither of us had mentioned Onu Gusti since he left us. Yet he was often on my mind, as surely he must have been on hers. Now there were just the two of us in the flower-strewn Alpine meadows. When we stopped to rest, Ema removed all of her clothes and lay down on the grass to tan her body in the hot sun while I busied myself picking the fragrant globeflowers, large as roses, which bloomed there in golden abundance.

On our way back, as we walked past the houses of the American administrators, a beautiful woman with dark curly hair and bright red lips motioned to me. She was obviously admiring the flowers I carried, sniffing the bouquet and saying words I didn't understand. Impulsively, I handed them to her.

"Thank you! Thank you!" she exclaimed in delight.

With a little wave to my mother, she took me by the hand into the house, pointed to a chair where I was to sit and held up her palm to indicate I should stay there while she went into another room. I am going to be rewarded for my generosity, I thought, so I waited patiently, swinging my legs and looking around. There was a picture on the opposite wall of a horse rearing up with a man wearing a large-brimmed hat sitting in the saddle.

I was just getting up to take a closer look when the front door opened. I gave the American soldier who entered my best smile and a curtsy but his face filled with anger as he pointed toward the door.

"OUT!" he commanded. "Get out you little rat. How the hell did you get in here?"

I didn't understand English but the import of his words was clear:

I am a poor child, a street urchin, a DP. I am looked upon as stupid and greedy, perhaps a thief. Though I didn't do anything wrong, I am guilty. I am no longer cute and respectable, smiled at by strangers or allowed to enter the houses of the wealthy.

I was humiliated and ashamed. And I never did receive my reward.

After that, I stopped going with Toomas to beg from the *Amis*, and spent the days with my mother, learning how to sew and knit. Ema taught me to baste, to hem, to fasten on buttons. She gave me some brown yarn and showed me how to cast on stitches and how to knit and purl.

One day the camp director distributed Red Cross packages. Everyone was given something. Ema came back with a pencil, a small pad of lined paper, a box of raisins with pictures of identical pretty women wearing big hats on either side, a toothbrush, orange vitamin pills, canned goods (Spam, sardines, beans, peas, succotash), and a green Army blanket. Also a Hershey bar. I couldn't remember ever tasting chocolate, as Toomas didn't share. Ema put it away for Christmas. She sharpened the pencil for me with a knife. I practised making letters on the new pad of paper.

The majority of Estonian DPs were educated city people—politicians, professionals, teachers, university students—all of them out-spoken anti-Communists in the forefront of the nationalistic fervour. By this time, they had hardened themselves to the big losses—their homes destroyed or left behind, their possessions gone, their loved ones dead or missing. There was no longer the comfort of belonging, the continuity of inheritance, the surety of aspirations based on past achievements. Their hopes and dreams had been torn asunder. They had to start again at zero. Perhaps even lower than that.

Yet life force is stronger than loss. You become accustomed to fear, to poverty. You make do. You act brave, even cheerful. Gradually hope returns. The worst might be over. Slowly you begin to assert your humanity. You walk in the mountains picking wild flowers to put in a tin can and set the bouquet on your suitcase. You play bridge to keep your mind active. You roll a *paberossi* from recycled tobacco carefully gleaned from discarded butts. (I gave my tin to my mother.) You steal corn from a nearby field and attempt to make liquor. You trade for small luxuries on the black market. You begin to organize: a chorus, a sports event, an acting group, a religious service.

There weren't enough Estonian children in this camp to start a school, but those who used to be teachers gave tutorials. A show was planned. Ema taught me a long narrative poem to perform. Dressed up as a little Tyrolean boy in lederhosen and a hat with a feather, I declaimed for a smiling audience who clapped loudly when I finished. Among other Estonians, I felt a renewed pride in myself. I could read, even though we had no books except the one my father gave me in Dresden. I learned to write words and put them together into sentences. I wrote a letter to Isa.

I was hoping that we could stay in Landeck forever. But though I didn't know it at the time, the atomic bomb had been dropped on Hiroshima. In September, the Japanese surrendered and World War II was over for everyone. To the victor go the spoils. The conquered lands were divided up. There was to be a French Zone, a British Zone, an American Zone, and a Russian Zone. A rumour took hold in the camp that Austria would be given to the Soviets.

Again there was the familiar sense of urgency, the scent of fear. We had to move westward where it was safer.

This time it was not my father who came to save me. It was Onu Gusti, driving a green car. He had come for Ema. I was merely the annoyance he must take along. He was taking us across the border to Germany, to a much bigger DP camp at Augsburg in the American Zone.

We said goodbye to Virve and to Toomas and to our other Estonian friends, knowing that we would probably never see them again.

"I don't want to go. Why do we have to go?" I cried.

"There will be lots of other Estonian children for you to play with. And you want to go to school, don't you?"

"Is Onu Gusti going to live with us?"

"No," Ema said, but she did not elaborate.

10.
Checkpoint

I FELL ASLEEP IN THE CAR. It was dark when I awoke. I stared at the back of Onu Gusti's head, his ears outlined in the headlights. Next to him in the front seat, Ema seemed to be asleep also, her head leaning heavily against the window. I turned to lie on my back to look at the moon, which was following us from Landeck along the curvy roads through the high mountains back to Germany, to the Hochfeld Camp in Augsburg.

"Get out the documents, Emps," Onu Gusti ordered, taking his hand off the steering wheel and reaching over to wake her. "We're at the checkpoint."

Ema stirred and began digging through a large purse, her *reticule.*

A white barrier with diagonal black stripes blocked the road. HALT said the sign. STOP. From within the bright oasis of electric light, the way ahead appeared black and ominous. A small hut stood to our left. Heat steamed from its walls. Smoke rose from the chimney.

"Are we there?" I asked, sitting up.

"Shush, child," Ema whispered.

She seemed nervous, fidgety, shuffling through the papers. The three of us stared at the building, waiting for someone to emerge and raise the barrier, but the door remained closed.

"Perhaps they don't know we are here," Onu Gusti proposed as we waited some more. Finally, not from exasperation, for that was no longer an option, but just to let someone know, he touched the horn lightly—a tentative and modest indication of our presence.

The door of the shack opened then, and a young soldier emerged, flushed with heat and straightening his jacket as he approached the car. I recognized the uniform—green with gold buttons, his small cap placed at a jaunty angle. An American. *Ami.*

Onu Gusti rolled down the window which had fogged up with our breath, and reached out the documents. Glancing at them quickly, the soldier cleared his throat and nodded. Without saying anything he handed them back, raised his chin to indicate we were to proceed and lifted the bar to let us through. Onu Gusti gave the papers to Ema and adjusted himself for the long drive ahead.

It was then he made his mistake.

He had forgotten he was a displaced person, a refugee in an occupied country defeated in war. The American soldier returned our papers. We were free to go. But where? There were no maps. We came from a small village in the distant mountains. Onu Gusti was transporting a woman and her child to safety. There was a fork in the road but no road signs. He wanted to make sure of the route, but the young man was already inside. He sounded the horn a second time.

Again, we waited.

There was still a chance to leave. The barrier had been raised. We could have driven off without pursuit. But this was a civilized land, and August Tamm was an educated man. All he wanted was to ask directions. Like most Estonians, Onu Gusti was stubborn. He pressed on the horn again. Loudly.

This time it was a different soldier. Older. Impatient. Annoyed. His hand rested on his revolver as he neared the car.

In halting English, thick with a German accent, Onu Gusti revealed our dilemma. Do we go here or there? This way or that way?

"Get out of the car," the soldier commanded. He shone a bright light into each of our faces. "Out! Out!" he indicated with his arm.

Obviously, he meant all three of us. He glanced briefly into the interior, then straightened up and pointed again with his flashlight.

"Open the trunk."

It was only mid-October but bitterly cold in the high mountain air under the dome of star-filled sky. Though wearing the new winter coat my mother had made, still I shivered. She wrapped her arms around me and pulled me close to keep me warm.

The soldier took everything out of the trunk, opened our suitcases, and strewed our belongings upon the pavement.

"American goods," he said, indicating the tin cans, the green blanket the same colour as his uniform, the Hershey bar.

"Red Cross," replied Onu Gusti.

The other soldier came out again to see what was going on.

Many Europeans spoke at least one or two languages in addition to their own, and most had studied English in high school. Ema approached the younger man. "Can the child please go inside where it is warm?" she managed to convey.

He nodded and led me up the steps into the hut.

In the centre of the room stood a potbellied woodstove, fired up. A bare light bulb dangled from a long cord. A wooden table carved with initials, an ashtray full of butts, a deck of cards, a half-empty bottle and some glasses, two hard chairs, a cot against the far wall. Slouched upon the cot, two blonde girls with shiny eyes and rosy faces, wearing bright red lipstick. I felt clumsy and exposed, but they never even gave me a glance, continuing to giggle and whisper together. From the window I saw Onu Gusti gesture and say something to the two soldiers as they searched inside the car, but they paid no more heed to him than these girls did to me. Ema was upset. I could tell by the way she sucked in her lower lip and wove her fingers together.

Shortly the younger of the two soldiers entered, his arms full of things he deposited on the table. The blanket, the tins of food—sardines and Spam. American goods. He took the Hershey bar Ema had been saving for Christmas to the German girls. I caught a whiff of chocolate as he slipped off the brown casing, unfolded the silver paper and broke off small squares to place between their red lips.

Standing numb by the stove. I blamed Onu Gusti. My mother was crying when she came in to take me back outside. We had been dismissed once again, free to enter the American Zone.

"Just a couple of young boys trying to impress the Frauleins," said Onu Gusti lightly, attempting to sweep away our helplessness. "I suspect they've been drinking. It could have been worse. At least they let us go."

I sat in the front seat between them. Ema said nothing. We were both crying. She held on to me tightly as we made our way through the winding roads out of the Alps and into Germany.

I would tell the story later, when I was well into my twenties and in graduate school:

The young guard at the checkpoint couldn't have been more than eighteen, the other one in his early twenties. Farm boys perhaps. From a small town maybe. Enlisted. Or drafted. Shipped to an unknown country, fighting a foreign war. Scared and swaggering. Growing up fast. Who can blame them for sneaking two nubile local girls into their hut? Inge and Gerta would surely be anticipating some reward for their compliance. They had accepted cigarettes and a few drinks from the bottle of whiskey the boys had been able to procure from the black market. Everything was going quite well, in fact, until a car horn sounded outside. There had been no traffic to speak of through this isolated mountain pass. They didn't expect anyone to be interrupting them in the middle of the night on this quiet road high in the Alps.

The younger of the two, lower in rank, speedily took care of the matter. But no sooner was he back inside than the horn sounded again.

What the hell?

The other soldier now took charge. Assessing the driver of the car, he knew right away what was what. They had been warned about this. There was a huge criminal element at loose in Europe. Racketeers. Stealing American goods intended for refugees. Selling them on the black market. Getting rich through the generosity of some and the misery of others. Like this sleazy guy with his heavy German accent, arrogant enough to blow his horn to ask directions. These people were defeated, for godsakes. They should act the part. They should show some respect.

"Get out of the car," he orders, his hand ready on the pistol.

A woman and a child cower in the background, but the man is still blabbering about something in his broken English.

The soldier feels an unexpected surge of anger. He wants to blow the goddamn Nazi's brains out or at least give him a good crack in the head. How dare he honk his horn like that? Who does he think he is? Some people just don't get it.

But he keeps his cool and does his duty. They had been told what to watch out for. They had permission to confiscate all American goods. Those were his orders. He reported almost everything he repossessed on the form he had to submit to his commanding officer. Luckily, he was able to control his temper, or there would have been one hell of a mess to clean up. He let the scum go. Even ended up giving the jerk directions to Augsburg. Everyone was happy. No harm done.

PART II
DISPLACED PERSONS

11.
Augsburg

THE HOCHFELD DP CAMP where Onu Gusti took us was not anything like the cluster of wooden barracks in the lush Alpine valley that we had left. Erected by the Nazis on the outskirts of the city of Augsburg to accommodate the workers of the Reich, it rose like a grey stone monolith from the surrounding farmland and consisted of rows of identical three-storey structures arranged in rectangular blocks with courtyards in the middle. When the Americans took possession, this entire complex was converted into one of the largest Baltic DP camps in Germany.

"Why did Onu Gusti bring us here?" I complained to my mother. "It's so ugly. It looks like a prison. I hate it."

"The bigger the *Laager*, the better the facilities," Ema said, without comforting me or elaborating further.

By the fall of 1946, over 150 DP camps had been established across Germany. With admirable foresight, the organizers gathered people of similar origin together. There were camps for Jews, for Poles, for Ukrainians, for the Balts. In Geislingen, there was a camp solely for Estonians. We called these camps *Laagers*, and they were places like no other, where total strangers lived in great intimacy like a large extended family joined by a common language, culture, and loss. Although the war was over, there was no expectation of going back home. A great percentage of those who fled had spoken out against Communist repression and injustice and fought alongside the enemy. Repatriation was impossible under Soviet rule. The Iron Curtain had fallen.

Communication between those who escaped and those who were left behind was curtailed for more than a decade. It became too painful to nurture the illusion that your particular loved ones had miraculously survived when so many millions had died. In order to exist, you had to deny remembrance. As the past was gone and the future not yet defined, *Laager* became our life. To say "We were in *Laager* together," implied the camaraderie of old soldiers from the same regiment who had survived a war. In *Laager*, we could lick our wounds in peace while putting our futures on hold. Billions of dollars of aid poured in. Food and medical facilities were provided. Certainly, it was not the best of circumstances, yet were never hungry or cold or in fear for our lives. A child's tears could be spent on the normal distresses of childhood.

Place defines memory. Smells, sounds, sights, people once known intimately and never seen again are permanently etched in the mind. When surroundings change, a new picture imprints itself. Those who live most of their lives where they are born often say they remember very little about their childhood, for it remains a part of an evolving mural in which colour, style, and atmosphere remain constant. A few isolated incidents might stand out in vivid detail, while the rest becomes immersed in the nostalgic collective of what used to be. Dramatic changes result in clearer recollections of time and place.

Three large blocks of buildings were designated only for Estonians, and it became easier to forget that we were living in a foreign country. Our room at 237 Hochfeld Strasse was on the ground floor. It was furnished with two wooden slat beds covered with striped mattresses, a small pot-bellied iron stove with an electric lightbulb hanging on a cord from the ceiling. Eight people lived in the two-bedroom apartment unit that had once served a single family. An elderly couple had the small room across the hallway; four young men, former soldiers, occupied the larger room next to ours. We all shared the WC and the kitchen. The inhabitants could either sign up for a fixed supply of dry ingredients and canned goods each week and cook their own meals, or line up at the communal dispensary with their containers to get a prepared meal each day. Once a week we had the use of the *Laager* bathhouse.

In any old photograph of a large gathering of DPs, Estonian children are easily identified if you know what to look for. You might expect to see blond hair, blue eyes, and round faces, but many Estonians do not fit this stereotype. Since the land had been occupied by foreign powers from the twelfth century onward, a variety of ancestors was inevitable. Even Isa, true patriot that he was, claimed to be a descendant of a Polish Count.

What distinguished us from the rest were not our physical features, but our caps, our scarves, our mittens, our sweaters, our socks, all bearing the repetitious motifs of Estonian folk art, and knit by our doting and industrious mothers. At any celebratory grouping you could pick us out, for not only children, but many of the mothers as well, would be dressed up in nationalistic finery that represented the various regions of the country. With the limited resources available, it took consummate skill and ingenuity, as well as innumerable hours, to recreate these costumes—the striped full skirts, the embroidered vests, the white blouses and aprons trimmed in delicate hand-crocheted lace, the woven belts, the fancy hats, the silver accoutrements.

After a long and devastating war, the pent-up creative energies of thousands of refugees had finally found release. A great percentage of the displaced were intellectuals: educators, artists, writers, students, professionals, all actively opposed to the Soviet regime. They had nothing left except their skills, their ingenuity, their ambition, and their nostalgia for a freedom that no longer existed. In *Laager* they once again had the opportunity to put their talents, knowledge, and capabilities to work. Since it was impossible to return, they took it upon themselves as a sacred duty to promote their national culture for future generations.

Laagers became as active as giant ant hills. Ministers conducted services, teachers taught in schools, writers composed memoirs, journalists penned virulent anti-communist editorials, publishers sold books and newspapers, artisans carved wood and embossed leather, jewellers fashioned brooches and chains from silver, musicians, actors, dancers, and gymnasts performed, poets wrote elegies about the lost homeland, sportsmen defended

Estonian honour in competitions with other *Laager* nationals. Every morning, the blue-black-and-white flag was hoisted in the Estonian sector by youthful troops of Scouts and Guides and was prominently displayed wherever Estonians gathered. All this effort was motivated by one unswerving purpose: to make sure their children would never forget their native language and the traditions of the homeland that might otherwise disappear forever under Soviet domination.

Ema had always been clever and industrious. During our stay in Hochfeld, she constantly improved our living quarters. She decorated old burlap bags with Estonian designs to make rugs that she hung up to cover the bare, dingy walls. She made fancy tiered curtains for our window from cheesecloth. She constructed two ottomans from wooden crates, stuffed them with the remnants of a discarded mattress and covered them with striped ticking to serve us as chairs. From confiscated cardboard and scraps of lumber, she built a closet in the corner of our room. She was a master of *kombineering*—combining and figuring—and never idle.

She was also inventive and artistic. She embroidered bright designs on the sweaters she knit for me—dogs and dolls and flowers and birds. The knee socks I wore were held up by colourful tassels. My new coat, fashioned from an old pair of army trousers, was not only warm, but also stylish, fastened on the side with three large brown buttons. And my hat was way over the top! Shaped like a Turkish fez, the four knitted panels were cleverly stitched together, standing stiff and upright to show off her fancy embroidery.

I was six when we moved to Hochfeld. An Estonian school had already been established, and my mother immediately made arrangements for me to attend. Although the traditional age for beginning school was eight, in *Laager* exceptions were made.

"I don't want to go. Why do I have to?" I whined. "I already know how to read."

"You have to learn as much as you can in life, Totsu," Ema told me. "You might have to leave everything else behind, but you can always bring your education with you."

I was more than just apprehensive; I was terrified. If I had been less timid, I would have run away and hid where no one could ever find me. My last experience of school revealed that no matter how much you had already learned, it meant nothing unless you also spoke the language. Later on, when we emigrated to America, I could again attest to this as a fact and present examples: Mr. Kuusik, a judge in Estonia, worked the remainder of his life in a doughnut factory; Dr. Nurme, a dentist, became a caregiver in a retirement home; Mr. Ploom, a student of theology, had a job in a factory; Mr. Tisur, the noted journalist, dug ditches. My mother herself was a waitress and then a housemaid for the first few years upon our arrival. Although my father claimed to be an instructor of fencing, that was part-time, in the evenings. In his regular daily job he worked as a janitor in an elementary school. It was their children's success that the older generation of immigrants worked for.

This time it would be different, Ema encouraged me. In *Laager* school everyone spoke Estonian. The children and the teachers. I had nothing to fear. I was her Totsu. I was smart and brave, and if I learned everything I could, I would always succeed in life.

12.
School

SOON AFTER WE SETTLED in Hochfeld *Laager*, Ema discovered that one of her former schoolmates from the *Gümnaasium* in Tallinn was also there. Although they hadn't known each other all that well, for Tädi Leena was several years older, when they met again, they hugged and cried together like sisters after a long and painful separation. Onu Karl and Tädi Leena had a son almost grown and a daughter my age, named Annie. She was puny and whiny with her entire family to coddle and spoil her. Right away I knew that I was smarter than she was.

But my mother was smarter than me.

"Annie attends school. She's in the first grade. She's been going for two months now. I bet she knows a lot more than you do," Ema told me.

"All right, I'll go," I conceded. But I pouted heavily about it for two whole days and kept my mother awake at night complaining of nightmares before the designated Monday morning arrived. Ema dressed me in my navy-blue skirt and white blouse, and since it was late October and there was a chill in the air, in my new coat and the tall, embroidered fez. Then we walked the two blocks of sidewalk to school.

I didn't want to go.

I didn't want to go.

Nevertheless, holding me firmly by the hand, she took me to the Grade One classroom and knocked on the door. From that point on, I was on my own. The room was filled with children sitting on benches behind long narrow tables. As the teacher led me to my place, everyone laughed. At my hat, I found out later, not at me. When I removed my coat and the object of ridicule, folding them neatly to serve as a cushion to sit upon as instructed, they began to look upon me as one of them. By the time we ate lunch and went outside into the courtyard for noontime recess, I was already feeling better about myself, knowing that I could read more fluently than the oldest girls in the back row and most of the boys.

As if to chastise me for my arrogance, the second humiliation occurred later that same day during mathematics class. I could say all the numbers up to one thousand and often practised counting before I fell asleep at night. I had no idea however, that numbers could also be used for computing. On the first afternoon of my arrival, we had a test. I neatly copied the rows of numbers from the blackboard and, showing off, wrote down as answers the biggest ones I could think of. All were marked wrong. My grade was a zero.

I was ashamed to face my mother. Ever since I was very little, I had been told how smart I was. Sometimes I was called stupid also, but it was much better to be smart, brave, cheerful, and obedient. And now, on my first day of real school, I had proved myself a failure. A zero. The lowest mark anyone could possibly get. I never did tell Ema about the hat. Upsetting her about the zero was enough.

She wasn't as angry as I thought she'd be. She explained to me about numbers and how they were used not only for counting but also for figuring. I practised all week, and, after that first horrible failure, things got better. The next time we had a test, I got a 5 (Excellent!). I put the hat in my pocket when my mother wasn't around. Eventually I lost it. These things happen and it is helpful to suffer a parent's disappointment at an early age in order to get through the rest of one's life. I lost a pair of mittens too.

After school, when the weather was fine, we often played Geese and Hounds or Skit. We needed chalk for Geese and Hounds, so we could only play if someone snitched a stub from school. The Geese would run off and leave a trail of arrows on the pavement or on the stone walls of the buildings. After counting slowly to one hundred, the Hounds would follow. When the Geese got tired of running, they would hide. Usually in a cellar stairway. It was scary. There were big rats in the cellars. I had seen them with my own eyes. Sometimes the Geese would flee into other parts of *Laager* where foreigners lived. I got really scared then, and the older kids would tell me to shush up or go home.

I liked Skit better. On the opposite side of our street, huge piles of tree-length logs were stacked—enough wood to heat all the rooms in *Laager*. In September, the men would begin to saw these into smaller pieces, which they would then split into chunks. Every room contained a small stove, and, if you wanted heat, you had to stand in line for your weekly allotment of wood. For much of the year however, the large woodpiles would become our private domain. We climbed over them and created forts and hideaways.

Older kids played Doctor and Nurse back there, with a lookout to shoo the younger ones away. We didn't care about their stupid games anyway. We liked playing Skit, taking turns being Director and either making up a story for the rest to act out or picking a folktale that was familiar to all. When it was my turn, I always chose *Turnip*. Turnip would squat down holding tight to a big log. The other players would then try to pull it up—Farmer, who would shout for Wife to help, who would call for Son, who would call for Horse, who would call for Cow, and so on, everyone tugging mightily until Turnip could hang on no longer and we would all tumble into a giggly heap.

Once the American soldiers introduced baseball, boys big and small would spend all their spare time around the playing field, while the girls occupied themselves with hopscotch or bounced balls against the stone walls of the buildings. In winter, everyone went sliding on the hill by the school. There weren't many sleds, but we all had stomachs in front and backsides behind which worked almost as well on the icy slope.

During the three and a half years I went to school in *Laager*, Annie-Mannie and I were the youngest in our class. We sat next to each other on the long bench in the front row. Tamara was the oldest. She was much taller than everyone else and already had breasts, which she tried to hide by stooping over. Due to the war, there had been no school for many children and especially not for refugees. I was lucky I was only six when we moved to

Hochfeld. Tamara was thirteen. She had never been taught to read and write, so she was put in Grade One. Perhaps she had lost her parents. She never played any of our games. She hardly ever spoke. No one paid much attention to her. She must have been very lonely.

Of all the boys who sat on the other side of the room, I liked Aldo the best. Aldo liked me too—I could tell because out at recess the other boys kept shoving him toward me—until a new girl, Mari, arrived. She had dark naturally curly hair and big brown eyes shaded by long eyelashes. Aldo began to pay attention to her instead. He even gave her a gift—a comb from a Red Cross package—and always managed to sit near her at the Saturday afternoon movies.

There was a new boy also, Ints. He was short and lithe with shiny black hair that hung in strands over his forehead. One dark eye stared straight ahead, the other strayed, looking for mischief. While standing in the corner (where he was put quite often as a punishment), he quickly turned his head and winked his wandering eye at me. Surely he must have been the offspring of a gypsy, for he stole my heart, and suddenly I didn't care about Aldo any more.

In school, we were taught Estonian language, Estonian history, writing, mathematics, religion, nature studies, geography, physical education, music, art, home skills, English, and German. There was a different teacher for every subject. My favourite was Proua Maas. She taught us English. She said that in English you had to say *aah* before you said anything else, like *aah boy, aah girl, aah man, aah woman. O boy*, meant something quite different. Sometimes you said: *the man, the woman, the boy.* None of little words had any meaning, so they couldn't be translated. It seemed odd having to say words that meant nothing. We also learned that most English words were not pronounced at all like they were spelled, so you couldn't read out loud unless you knew how to say the word even if you knew what it meant.

Estonian seemed so clear and simple in comparison. All the words you spoke meant something and were spelled exactly as they sounded. I didn't know there was a subject called *Spelling* until we moved to America. Eventually I came to realize, however, that even our own language has its eccentricities: there is no gender; there are no prepositions (instead the nouns change, as do the modifiers, so irregularly that often only the first letter of the word remains constant); there is no future tense. It is a language almost impossible to learn for anyone not born Estonian. But the intricacies of a native language, like the attitudes and customs assimilated in childhood, become such an integral part of one's reality that it requires a total immersion into a different culture to recognize just how peculiar they really are.

Pr. Maas didn't just teach vocabulary, she also instructed us in the flow of the language. Her method was simple. She read to us out loud, translating everything she read. By listening, we learned. The last book I remember her reading to us was *Uncle Tom's Cabin*. When I found out that we were going to America, I was apprehensive. It seemed like such a cruel country, filled with violence, and intolerant of those who were different. Yet most Americans we met turned out to be helpful and kind, and though it took me a while to learn to speak English, I understood very quickly what was said to me. I have Pr. Maas to thank for that.

13.
Kati

IT DIDN'T TAKE ME LONG to realize why Onu Gusti had brought us to Augsburg, for he lived close by in Geislingen *Laager* with his family, and came to visit us often. I was also smart enough by then to figure out why he didn't move us there, even though it was the best *Laager* of all, where nearly five thousand Estonians lived in confiscated private houses with gardens and back yards. Isa ended up much further away, in the Lübeck *Laager* on the northern coast. Since they arrived in Germany separately, my mother and father were not designated as a family unit and were thus not obligated to sign up together.

We had been at Hochfeld for several months when a letter arrived addressed to me:

My dear darling little daughter,

How I have missed you these past few years, not knowing how you and your mother were getting by. For some of that time, I thought I myself was dying and spent many months in hospital. But now I am well again and continue my life in Lübeck.

Do you remember when we last saw each other in Dresden? You were just a little tyke then, but still strong enough to knock your old man over when we were boxing. Only five, and already you could read. Do you still have the book I made for you?

Our homeland no longer belongs to us, and this is very sad. We fought long and hard to preserve our independence and lost only because those we thought our friends did not stand by us. Someday we will go back to a free Estonia with our heads held high, and you can always be proud that you are the daughter of an Estonian soldier.

I am still wearing a uniform, but not the same colour as before. This one is black. Now I am working for the Americans. No longer can I fight for our ravaged homeland, but am entrusted with guard duty and I also keep order in Laager.

Please give my best regards to your mother, and I hope you both are well.

From the DP *camp in Lübeck, with deepest regards and the greatest love,*

Your devoted, Isa

The letter was in Estonian of course, so I could read all the words. When I showed it to my mother, she made a noise of contempt from deep in her throat—*Ecchh*—but said nothing more.

I cut the stamps off the envelope for my collection, and, since we were learning to use a pen and ink in school, I could hardly wait to write back. It was a messy business with the tools I had—a penholder with a detachable nib that had to be constantly dipped into the jar of ink. There were quite a few errant spots, some agonizing blots, and disastrous spills. The forefinger and thumb of my right hand were stained a lovely bright purple for a considerable time as a badge of my accomplishment.

He would come to see me as soon as he was able to get a car, Isa wrote back, and since he couldn't be with us, he had found a little puppy named Kati to keep him company.

In subsequent letters, he told me about her—how smart and cute she was, and the tricks he was teaching her. She would sit at his command and lie down and roll over and shake hands, and she was only six months old! She had a leather collar and a leash, and he took her for walks around the city of Lübeck, and at night she went with him to patrol the *Laager*. He had told Kati all about me, he said—how smart and pretty I was, and how much I loved dogs. At the end of his letters he would sign both of their names—his own and Kati's paw print in ink.

I loved dogs ever since I had seen them performing in the puppet theatre when we lived in Dresden. I wanted a dog more than anything in the whole entire world, but Ema said that this was a ridiculous wish. Couldn't I see that she had enough trouble trying to feed and dress and take care of a child all by herself? *Dogs have to eat too,* she said. *A DP camp is no place for a dog,* she said.

When summer came, my father did as he promised. He had acquired an old, beat-up military car and driven the long distance from Lübeck to visit us. He looked different. Not nearly so big or so tall as I remembered. But still very strong and handsome and much nicer looking than Onu Gusti. He took me in his arms the way he used to when I was little and threw me up into the air. I wasn't scared of him anymore. He was a lot jollier than my mother. And the most wonderful thing of all—he brought Kati with him!

Kati was beautiful. She had short tan fur. Her ears, tipped with dark tufts, lifted up whenever anyone spoke to her. She gave me her paw to say hello, and she licked me on the nose. Right away I loved her. I couldn't stop hugging her. Isa put on her leash and allowed me to take her outside for a walk. Kati stayed right by my side. All the other kids on the block came to pat her, and I told them that Kati belonged to me. When we got back, Isa brought a bowl from the car and I gave her water. Ema folded up an old blanket and placed it on the floor beside the stove where Kati could sleep.

Isa also spent the night in our room. There were only the two narrow beds, so he slept with my mother. In the morning when I woke up, she had already gone to her job, but he was still there, snoring with his mouth open, one bare hairy leg hanging outside the covers. I was astounded that Ema could have fit into such a small space between the bulk of his immense body and the unyielding wall. Before I left for school, I hugged Kati good-bye and gave her the bread and Spam I was supposed to have for lunch. I didn't want her to leave, ever. All day long I couldn't stop thinking about her.

When I got home, Isa's car was gone. But as I opened the

door to our room, there was a big surprise. Kati was still there, wagging her tail and running over to lick my face. A note lay on my pillow:

> *My dear darling daughter,*
> *I know how much you love Kati and how much she loves you, so I am leaving her for you as a present. Take good care of her. She is a fine and intelligent dog, and she will keep you company. I will try to visit again soon.*
> *With greatest affection,*
> *Your devoted, Isa*

My happiness lasted only until Ema arrived home from work. She was furious.

"He's like a child," she said. "He's totally irresponsible. Don't you realize how hard it is for me to keep you fed? He never gives you a thing. I have to do it all. What would happen to you if I wasn't around, eh? Yet you think he is so wonderful. He didn't give you this dog because he loves you, child. He's tired of it. He intended to leave it here all along. Who's going to feed it? Who's going to take care of it?"

"I will," I said in a small voice through my tears. "I'll share my food. I'll take her for walks every day. I promise."

The dog knew something was wrong. Her large brown eyes looked at each of us in turn.

My mother was crying now too. She took the note Isa had left, ripped it up into small pieces, and threw the pieces into the stove.

"All right, Tita," she said. "You *will* be responsible. But none of our food goes to this dog. It will be your job to stand at the end of the line at the soup kitchen every day, and, after everyone has been served, you can beg for what is left. Do you understand?"

I nodded, snuffling.

That same evening, I walked the six blocks to the *Laager* kitchen, carrying one of the large tin cans which had been handed out to the DPs and which we called *Trumans*. For a long time I stood in line and waited. After everyone else had been served, I went up to the counter. It was humiliating, and I was scared, but I had to do it. For Kati.

"Please, Proua, if you have any leftovers you can spare, could I have a little bit? It's for my dog."

Estonians are very proud. We hate to ask for anything except information. Without saying a word but looking at me sternly, the woman ladled the dregs of green pea soup into my *Truman*.

This became my nightly chore for some time.

At first, I took great pleasure in putting the leash on Kati and showing her off around the Estonian sector. Everyone stopped to talk to her. She was so gentle and lovable that she would even allow me to dress her up in a bonnet and wheel her around in an old baby carriage that someone had left in the front hallway. But after a while it got to be a nuisance to take her everywhere instead of being free to play my own games. I especially hated going to the soup kitchen. Kati wasn't doing so well either. She became skinny. Her hair fell out. Often she vomited and had diarrhea, and it was my job to clean it up. At night when my mother went to bed, she would let Kati outside for a run. Kati was a smart and loyal dog. She would always be waiting at the door of 237 Hochfeld in the morning.

I loved her with all my heart, but sometimes I got impatient because it was not as much fun having a dog as I thought it would be. Lots of times Kati just lay around looking miserable. One night when my mother was at choir practice, I decided to give my dog some training.

"Kati," I called. "Come here."

Kati opened one eye and looked at me as if to say, "Can't you see I'm trying to sleep. What do you want me to come there for?"

"Kati, come here!" I commanded once again. Very slowly Kati rose from her mat and obediently ambled over, not wagging her tail. "When I say come, you COME," I said loudly, pinching her ear until she whined.

After she lay back down, I made her practise several more times. Each time Kati would rise up from her resting place, but not quickly enough for the impatient and cruel little mistress.

"If you came right away, I wouldn't have to pinch you," I told her, pinching harder.

I don't think she understood, and I felt horrible afterwards. When Onu Gusti next came to visit, bringing me a box of biscuits,

I felt so guilty that I shared them with Kati. Ema saw, but for some reason she didn't say anything.

The next morning when we were having breakfast in the kitchen, she told me that Onu Gusti had come to take Kati away.

"No! no," I cried. "He can't have her. What will I tell my father?"

"You don't have to tell your father anything," Ema said. "I'll take care of that part."

She explained once again how impossible it was for us to take care of a dog in a DP camp. Surely I could see myself how skinny and sickly Kati was. Also the camp administrator told her at work that there had been complaints from some neighbouring farmers that their chickens were being killed. They suspected a dog was responsible. Onu Gusti had found a home for Kati with some Americans, Ema told me. This was for her own good, she said.

Before I left for school, I opened the window of our room, dragging Kati off her mat to show her. "If Onu Gusti comes, you jump out and run away," I instructed. Then I hugged and kissed her and gave her the rest of the biscuits.

That afternoon when I got home, Kati was gone. So was her leash that used to hang on a nail by the door. The window was shut. When Ema returned from work, she repeated her story about Kati's wonderful new life with the rich Americans. I had to believe her, for I certainly could not have withstood the truth.

I can hardly bear thinking of it now.

14.
Hochfeld 237

THE COUPLE WHO LIVED across the hall from us was always kind to me, but ever since we first moved into Hochfeld 237, my mother had warned me to keep away from the four young men in the room next door. They had been soldiers but not Freedom Fighters like Isa. As schoolboys in Estonia, they were conscripted by the occupying Nazis to serve in the German army. The dark-haired one had a missing leg, the other two had each lost an arm, the youngest had all his limbs, but was funny in the head. That's what Ema said, and it seemed to be true for he often laughed or sometimes cried at nothing. Most of the time they were quiet and polite, unless they were able to get liquor, which became much more frequent after the men in the next building started making vodka in the cellar. Whenever they got drunk we could hear them through the thin wall singing sad songs about the lost homeland. Sometimes they shouted bad words: *KURAT! SITT!* There would be vomit in the WC and in the hallway. One of them peed in the old couple's room by mistake. They always apologized after.

Shortly before Christmas, the nicer of the two one-armed men approached my mother to ask a favour: "Please, Proua, could you keep this bottle in your room and promise not give it to us under any circumstances, even if we beg you for it, so we'll have something to celebrate the holiday."

Ema said no at first—she was not about to take responsibility for anything like that, not under any circumstances—but he looked so sad with his brown puppy-dog eyes that she finally relented. They were only young boys after all, barely out of their teens, I heard her explain to Tädi Leena afterwards. Beneath the crust of her strong opinions and judgements, my mother was sometimes quite soft-hearted.

About that same time, I got sick with the mumps. My cheeks puffed up on both sides. I had a fever and couldn't go to school. When Ema went to work in the morning, she left a glass of water and some soup for my lunch, gave strict orders to keep the door locked, to stay in bed, and to use the *Truman* if I had to pee.

For a long while I played with my paper dolls among the hills and valleys of the bedclothes. Then I sang all the songs I knew. After that I ate a few spoonfuls of soup and slept for a bit until I heard a noise that made me sit straight up in bed. Someone was rattling the door handle. I put the blanket over my head like I used to in Tallinn so if the Communists came they would take me for a pile of rumpled old clothes and leave me be. The pounding on the door got louder. The handle rattled again. I heard a man's voice cursing: "KURAT!" When everything remained quiet for some time, I dared to peer out from under my blanket. The door was secure, but when I turned my head the other way, I saw a face pressed against the window. Opening my mouth to scream, I recognized the one-armed soldier from the room next door.

He tapped on the glass and waggled the fingers of his hand at me to come closer.

"Your mother has something of ours," I could hear him hollering through the glass.

"She isn't here," I called back.

"Open the window," he urged, indicating with his arm how I should go about it.

Ema hadn't left instructions about the window. I drew the latch and stood aside as he clambered in.

"You're a good little girl", he said, giving me the hated head-ruffle, before grabbing a bottle that was in plain sight beside the stove. He cradled it under his arm and hopped out.

I closed the window and climbed back under the covers as if nothing had happened, but Ema noticed right away that the bottle was missing. She was furious. She had had enough of living next door to drunken louts. She had a young daughter to protect. How dare he force her out of bed to open the window in the middle of winter? The child had a fever, for heaven's sake. She could have come down with pneumonia again. She'd had it once before already. She almost died then. Her lungs may have been permanently weakened.

When Ema was determined, there was no standing in her way. She worked at the Camp Administration Office and knew where to present her case. Not long after, we moved to the second floor of Hochfeld 237 into a bigger room that we had to share with Preili Sütt. She seemed a nice enough young girl, my mother said. Also, someone would be around to keep an eye on me when she herself was at work.

There were two other children in this apartment. One was a little girl, Maimu Asti, who was not yet in school. Her father had been an officer in the Estonian army, but had never run into Isa. Because of the war, Härra Asti had lost contact with his wife and didn't even know he had a daughter until Maimu was four years old and the family reunited in Augsburg. I learned this later, for my mother and the Astis remained lifelong friends.

Jaak and his mother lived in the other small room. Jaak was older than I. He had been injured during a bombardment and was missing most of his face. After a while I got used to his appearance, but I never liked him. He was mean, and so was his mother. We had to share the kitchen and the bathroom, but she never wanted to share anything else.

The four young soldiers, our former neighbours, also left soon after we moved upstairs. For months, there had been rumours that all the *Laagers* were going to be screened for undesirables. Everyone's papers were going to be checked. Men who had served in the German Army would be scrutinized before a board of examiners, and anyone suspected of collaborating with the Nazis during the war would be evicted from the DP camps. It was a desperate situation for many. Screened out of *Laager*, they might be forced to return to the homeland where they would surely be killed by the Communists or sent to work camps in Siberia. Even if allowed to remain in Germany, how could they sustain themselves? Only German citizens were issued food stamps and working papers.

Those who had fought with the Estonian army, like my father and Hr. Asti were safe from the screenings. Although their units sided with Germans against Communists, they were designated as a foreign legion. Isa was a legionnaire; the German uniform he was forced to wear bore the Estonian insignia. All those who had been conscripted into the German army, however, were suspect. Some had elected to serve with the SS to better their situation. Inside their left arm, above the elbow, they bore the dreaded tattoo. The youngest of the soldiers in Hochfeld 237 had this mark. I had seen it myself, the dark Runic letters, one slightly above the other, as he tried to erase them at the kitchen sink with lemons, with bleach, with various other solutions he had heard about. Nothing worked. He was imprinted forever.

The other three were luckier. Two had lost the offending arm during the war. The one with the missing leg served in the labour force and had no tattoo. Were they all screened out of *Laager*? I wondered. Or did they move elsewhere, as we had? Ema doesn't recall, but I remember stories I wasn't supposed to hear about men putting belts around their necks and hanging themselves from doorways.

Onu Gusti came to visit sometimes on weekends. Prl. Sütt was often gone then, and I knew full well that he wanted me out of the way also so he could be alone with Ema. But I had to protect my own interests and thus stuck to him like a tick in springtime. Even after I was put to bed, I kept an eye on them, trying my best to stay awake, lifting my weary head to rest its weight upon my elbow, attempting to peer with sleepy eyes through the crack behind the stacked-up wooden crates which separated my bed from my mother's and served us as a bureau. From there, I saw nothing. At the other end, only their ankles and feet were visible. Every once in a while, her bed would creak, and I was sure I heard the disgusting slurpy plops of kissing.

Always an obedient child, I didn't dare get up to take a closer look. All I could do was chew off my fingernails as I tried to keep track of their every move. Everyone in the block knew what they were doing, my friend Helle said, with that special little smirk she reserved for filthy things. I hated my mother then, same as I did Onu Gusti. But I loved her also, and when Onu Gusti left, I would feel guilty about my mean thoughts and crawl into her lap to be cuddled. I knew it pleased her when I did that because usually I didn't like to be touched by her or anyone else.

Ema believed in education, persistence, and hard work. Although she liked Prl. Sütt well enough, I was not to snoop around and listen to what she and her friends talked about. It was nothing little girls should be interested in. My job was to study hard and do well in school and to make my mother proud. Did I understand?

Prl. Sütt, on the other hand, thought it was more important to be in the right place at the right time, so she curled her blonde hair up in rags every Saturday morning and went to places where there was dancing on Saturday nights. Often she would not return until the following afternoon. She and her girlfriends indulged in long discussions laced with the same sort of suppressed hilarity that I had come to recognize whenever women whispered about certain things children were not supposed to know. But Prl. Sütt didn't care what I overheard, and indeed, their chatter dealt with nothing more sinister than who they had spent time with on Saturday night, who said what and who danced the best, who was the most handsome, and which *Amis* they hoped to meet again. Prl. Sütt was generous in every way. Not only did she share her emotions and hopes and fears and laughter, but her material acquisitions as well. Often she brought back nylon stockings, cigarettes, and chocolate, which she usually gave to me. She liked the dark-skinned soldiers the most. They were the best dancers, she said, spent their money freely, and gave the nicest gifts. I myself also thought they were the handsomest of all the *Amis*. When I grew up, I told Ema, I was going to marry a Negro. She raised no objections to that. Her prejudices had not yet extended to the New World.

One afternoon when I came home from school, Prl. Sütt and a man from the next building were lying together in her bed. Onu Gusti always lay down on my mother's bed with her, so this did not seem in any way extraordinary. Where else was someone supposed to be? My mother had not yet made our two striped ottomans, and the room was furnished with the three single beds, our two suitcases under the blue checkered tablecloth, the crates where we kept our stuff, and the pot-bellied iron stove to provide heat in winter.

Prl. Sütt wasn't usually friendly with the men from *Laager*. She wanted an American or a Canadian to marry. I don't know why I told my mother.

"This man, Ennis, comes to our room practically every afternoon before you get home and they giggle and tickle each other in Prl. Sütt's bed," I said, trying to make it sound as though I was happy they were having so much fun and Ema should be too. Deep inside I knew I was tattling. I suspect it had something to do with what Helle had told me about my mother and Onu Gusti and what my mother always said herself—*Men are disgusting, remember that, Tita.*

Ema had words with Prl. Sütt then, out of my hearing, and when a single room became available on the third floor, we moved again.

As I think of her now, I see a big-boned, clumsy, raw girl with wavy blonde hair and large full lips, which would often widen into a toothy smile. Preili Sütt. Coping by herself in a world gone insane, keeping her own survival firmly in mind. She was uncalculating, but strong-willed and focused, using every bit of her young energy to go after what she wanted.

Thirty years later, my mother got a letter from her. She had tracked down Ema by contacting the Estonian Consulate in New York City. She finally did marry her soldier, she wrote, and emigrated to a ranch in Montana, where she rode horses, roped cattle, and busied herself raising a passel of blue-eyed youngsters. She apologized for not writing in Estonian; she had misplaced almost every blasted word of her native language, she said. But she remembered Ema, who was like family to her when she was hardly more than a child in the Hochfeld DP Camp (though people did grow up fast in those times). She had no one left on her side, she said, whereas her husband seemed to be related to nearly every person in the whole county. My mother wrote back and sent Christmas cards for years, but never did hear from Prl. Sütt again.

What was it, I wondered, that prompted this woman to go to all that trouble to make the initial contact and then never pursue it? Justification? Curiosity? A yearning to connect to the past? Or to reveal the end of her story to the only other person in the world who understood about the beginning, with no need to say anything more.

15.
Laager

A GREAT DEAL OF TIME, effort, and energy was expended in DP camps by the older generation to make up for the trauma and deprivation that children had suffered during the war. Although much was done for us, much was also expected. We had survived; now we had to overcome—educationally, creatively, culturally, physically, and emotionally. It did no good to delve into the past to regret our losses and misfortunes. What was gone was gone. One had to do the best with what one had. This attitude certainly helped us thrive, although the deeper, untreatable wounds left scars that remained for the rest of our lives.

Laager was a waiting room, a temporary holding place for the homeless. Our future was yet to be determined. For children, however, the here-and-now is always more potent than the there-and-then, and by the time we moved to the third floor of Hochfeld 237, my identity had been established.

Since we stayed in Augsburg for nearly four years, the chronology of this time in my remembrance becomes somewhat haphazard. I was in Grade One, then Grade Two, then Grade Three. First I liked Aldo, but after Mari replaced me in his affections, I liked Ints. I had a pen, a bottle of purple ink, and notebooks filled with my own writing. I was good in mathematics: I could add and subtract three digit numbers and memorized the multiplication tables. I had a set of coloured pencils, a box of twelve crayons that I got from a Red Cross package, and a tin with little squares of watercolour paint. I was not a talented artist; Ema was much better. I had two large collections of paper dolls— for fashion and for play. I took piano lessons from Hr. Puu, and could play "Für

Elise" without mistakes. I was getting good at sewing: I knew how to baste, hem, and stitch up seams. I could also fasten on buttons and hooks, darn socks, and do some fancy embroidery—the leaf, the satin stitch, the French knot. I was knitting a vest for myself out of brown yarn. The whole back and half of the front were finished before we moved from *Laager* and it got thrown out with a lot of the other stuff we left behind.

Whenever I got a letter from my father, I cut out the stamp and soaked it in a glass of warm water to dissolve the glue. Removing it carefully with tweezers, I let it dry before storing it in my stamp album. I owned a set of wooden pick-up sticks of various thicknesses, painted with different coloured stripes to signify worth for scoring. Consummate skill was required to take one stick from the pile without disturbing the rest. I also had a high-bouncing red ball, a lucky hopscotch stone, a metal hoop from a bicycle tire that I pushed with a stick along the pavement, a bag full of marbles, and a pair of roller skates that fastened to the bottom edge of my shoes. They were highly coveted in the neighbourhood. We took turns skating on the sidewalk in front of our building. I was in charge of who borrowed the skates.

My mother owned two decks of cards, and I was allowed to use them for building card houses. She used them for bridge or to play double solitaire with Tädi Leena. Also sometimes for fortune telling when Proua Nelli visited. Often in the evenings, women came to our room to play cards. Two sat on one bed and two on the other with the suitcase table in between. Falling asleep behind the bulk of their unheeding backsides, their words became my lullaby: *two spades, three clubs, four no trump, six clubs, double, re-double, pass, pass.*

I had several new books—Christmas and birthday gifts. They were written in Estonian, printed in Sweden, and shipped to our DP camp in Germany. My mother had some books too. I read them all many times, both hers and mine. Sometimes Ema brought American funny papers home from work and we cuddled together on her bed to look at the comic strips: *Little Lulu, Donald Duck, Mickey Mouse*. She translated the stories for me.

American movies were shown to DP children on Saturday afternoons. I went because Helle and Annie-Mannie did, but I didn't like it. There was always a huge crowd of all ages and nationalities, loud and rowdy. The films too were scary— I still remember a werewolf's enormous paws walking down a long dark passageway to stalk victims and a scene where two lovers jumped from a cliff to their death because a troop of whooping savages was chasing them. I often put my hands over my eyes and had nightmares afterwards.

Food was a great preoccupation in *Laager*, but not very important to me. Due to my mother's solicitude, I had never felt hunger. It was possible to get our daily supply from the soup kitchen in our *Truman,* but Ema always preferred weekly rations so she could prepare our meals herself. We were given a loaf of sliced white bread, a jar of peanut butter (which we called *monkey sweat*), a can of Spam, powdered milk, and other items I don't recall. Everyone who worked for the Americans, like my mother, was paid in cigarettes as well as money. The German mark had become worthless, but with cigarettes, one could buy practically anything. Ema's pay was 200 German marks and two packs of Chesterfields per month. She smoked one pack, making it last by cutting the cigarettes in fourths and smoking the stubs in a cigarette holder. With the other pack, she traded and was able to supplement our food supply by buying things from nearby farms or on the black market.

I recall a few particularly memorable items from our menu:

Koogel-moogel: a raw egg beat up with sugar as a special treat for me.

Cauliflower soup: a disaster; filled with bugs that floated on top like flakes of pepper. *Cooked bugs are good for you*, Ema insisted. *Protein.*

Monkey sweat on white bread: Estonians have two words for bread: *leib*—dark, every-day, hardy bread, and *sai*—white, sweet special bread. In *Laager* we got American *sai*, which you could squish into a ball between your fingers like a ball of soft dough and which had no taste at all.

Cherries: after we ate a few, I bit one in half to discover a fat white worm inside. Thereafter we found a worm in every single one. Undaunted, Ema cut out the worms and we ate the cherries. A plateful of worms remained on the table like squirming grains of rice. I was hoping she was truthful when she said she would throw these away, but that night I scrutinized my dinner carefully just in case.

Cod-liver oil: a daily dose to keep me healthy. During the process, bravery was indoctrinated as a positive attribute in life. I had to swallow a tablespoon of the vile stuff every morning without making a fuss.

Orange Vitamin pill: one every morning, tasted for hours in every burp thereafter.

Pancakes: my favourite; flipped in the frying pan by a skilful cook, and rolled up like crepes by a skilful eater.

At Christmas we had *sült, vorst, kringel,* and *pipparkook.* At Easter we had hardboiled eggs that Ema coloured with onion skins or decorated with designs of chicks and bunnies using my watercolours.

Like most Estonian girls between the ages of six and ten, I was a *Hellake.* Dressed in dark blue skirts and blouses with light blue neckerchiefs, we had meetings once a week. We also wore the uniforms on weekends when we marched behind the Scouts and Guides to the centre of the courtyard square for the raising and lowering our blue-black-and white flag. The older kids saluted with three fingers, we saluted with two, and there was a group of pre-schoolers who didn't yet have uniforms but wore neckerchiefs and were allowed to salute with one finger.

My greatest triumph in *Laager* came when I was chosen to play the lead role in a three-act play that the theatre society put on to entertain the children at Christmas. Dressed in a white, furry costume with long ears and a fluffy tail, I was *Jänku-Jukku,* a rabbit, the youngest member of the cast and the star of the show. The play was a huge success, and for a long while I basked in the glow of my fame.

But nothing lasts forever.

16.
Higher Education

DURING THE TWENTY YEARS of Estonian independence between the two World Wars, a national singing festival was held each year in Tallinn. Outfitted in traditional attire, choral groups from every corner of the land joined together to perform the songs each had practised separately during the year. After DP camps were established, this celebration continued in exile. During the summer *of* 1948, Hochfeld *Laager* hosted the event. There was a grand parade of singers who came from *Laagers* all over Germany with everyone dressed in national costumes marching through the city of Augsburg to the large amphitheatre where the concert was to be held.

Men had it easy—dark pants tucked into woollen knee socks, a white shirt trimmed with lace or embroidery, a woven belt of traditional design. Acquiring the proper woman's outfit was much more difficult, although some had actually managed to bring the authentic clothing with them when they escaped. For most, however, it took months of planning and intricate needlework to recreate an acceptable facsimile.

Children took no part in the performance, but Ema decided to make a national costume for me anyway. Expressing her partiality for fanciful headgear once again, she elected to reproduce the traditional dress of the Muhu region—its most outstanding feature being an enormous flared hat. This she fashioned from cardboard that she covered with white fabric and colourful embroidery. Out of old parachute silk, she sewed a white blouse with puffy sleeves, edging the collar and cuffs in handmade lace. It was topped by an intricately embroidered vest. For the skirt, she used long cotton strips stitched onto a woollen background to approximate a striped weave, and from a distance it was hard to tell the difference. A hand-woven belt, a silver *sõlg*, white knee-socks, and a pair of new shoes completed the outfit. I wore it for the first time on the day of the singing festival and, while we remained in *Laager*, to every celebratory function thereafter.

For herself, she was able to borrow an authentic ensemble—quite simple in comparison with some—consisting of a woven striped skirt, an apron trimmed in lace, and an embroidered white blouse. She marched in front of the Hochfeld Women's Chorus as the flag bearer. Those few who didn't have access to a costume, like Preili Sütt, wore a white dresses with an Estonian belt wrapped around their waists. In my beautiful new outfit, I walked close to the curb along with the singers, keeping in step with Ema. Crowds of people came to watch the long column of Estonian singers parade through the streets. The concert began with the national anthem. There were thousands of spectators and many a tearful face listening to the old songs. I was proud to be an Estonian.

It was a common practice at the time to present flowers to the conductor and to the soloists at the conclusion of every performance. Children dressed in traditional costumes were chosen to hand out the bouquets. I had been selected for this honour and assigned to the most important personage of all, the conductor. Clutching large bunches of flowers, the line of children, arranged from youngest to oldest, waited impatiently in the wings for the final number to end. When the burst of applause finally quieted, being the youngest and the first in line, I walked self-consciously across the enormous stage and offered up my bouquet to the man standing in front of the vast group of singers.

"Not yet," he whispered crossly, motioning me away, for he had just raised his baton for the encore. It was only then that I realized no one else had followed me. The concert wasn't over. There was a smattering of laughter from the audience as I stood in confusion and despair not knowing what to do. Finally I placed the flowers on the floor behind the heels of the man's well-polished black shoes, and, with as much dignity as I could muster, crossed to the opposite side of the vast stage as we had been told to do. There, alone and in great misery, I waited through two more encores.

When it was definitely all over, the rest of the bouquets were distributed. But the woman in charge wasn't as angry as I had expected. "You were just too eager. Everyone thought it was cute," she said. Even Ema offered comfort as I cried bitter tears over my disgrace, certain that my days of glory were ended forever.

That evening there was a huge gathering for all the participating singers, which lasted late into the night. Since Ema and Tädi Leena were both attending, Annie-Mannie was allowed to sleep over to keep me company. Although I didn't like her all that much, I was happy not to be alone. We could draw outfits for our paper dolls. We could play cards. We could stay up as late as we wanted.

At first we had a game of pick-up-sticks. After that we built houses of cards. Then we lay down on my bed and took turns telling stories. I told the one about a beautiful princess who was going to be sacrificed to the King of the Night. Annie told the one about a beautiful princess with a pea under her mattress. Then she suggested we play *Bride and Groom* and showed me how. First we had to kiss, which made us giggle. Then we had to touch tongues, which was repulsive and slimy. After that we got really silly and began to tickle each other, even in our private places. Somehow we both knew that what we were doing was naughty, something we definitely shouldn't tell our mothers about. Later that night Annie-Mannie peed the bed. She blamed me, but anyone could tell it was her. There was a big puddle right through the mattress on her side.

Shortly thereafter my mother began my sexual education.

Whenever I had my knees up under the blanket, she would say, "Put your knees down, Tita," then ask me where my hands were.

"Right here," I would reply, surprised at the question, holding both of them up to prove it.

"Keep them on top of the covers where I can see them. Do you understand?"

It was all very puzzling. Where would they be except attached to my arms as usual? And why would she want to see them? "How come?" I finally dared to ask.

"For health reasons," she said. "And remember this, Tita—the only time you ever touch yourself in the private place is to wipe it or wash it."

I knew then, that as usual, Annie-Mannie had tattled. My mother never mentioned the incident directly, but it was obvious that I should be ashamed about what we had done. And I was.

I began to spend most of my time with Helle after that.

"Why aren't you playing with Annie anymore? She's such a nice little girl," Ema would urge.

"Because Annie-Mannie tattles about everything," I wanted to reply, but I kept that to myself.

I also made friends with two older girls who lived in our block, red-haired Lydia and rough-mouthed Tasha. Neither of them had fathers, but both had younger siblings, snot-nosed toddlers that followed them everywhere. Ema didn't like either of these girls. "They have Russian features," she said. Nor did she approve of their mothers, although she didn't tell me why.

There weren't very many babies in *Laager*, and only one was born during the whole time we lived there as far as I knew. My piano teacher, Härra Puu, had a wedding, and not long thereafter his wife gave birth to a baby boy. This was quite an event for everyone. All the little girls who took piano lessons were very excited about Edu-Rein. Proua Puu would sometimes take him out of the box where he slept bundled in a light blue flannel blanket and show him to us. I asked permission to bring my friend Helle to my lesson so she could see him also. Helle was in love with babies.

That Christmas, Helle and I both received dolls. Right away Helle named hers Edu-Rein. I wished I would have thought of it first, but Helle was a much better mother to her doll, so she deserved to have the name. She changed his nappies, dressed him in little shirts and nighties, cuddled him, and cooed to him as if he truly was a real little baby. Helle's own baby brother had died during the war, so she had experience that I lacked.

In actual fact, I didn't care for babies all that much, for I had this horrible fear, never revealed, that Ema and Onu Gusti would someday have a baby whom she would love much more than she ever loved me. If that happened, I vowed to put a belt around my neck and hang myself from a doorway like the men who were screened out of *Laager*. Then Ema would be sorry and it would serve her right.

Biting on her lower lip and staring gleefully at me out of the black-ringed sockets of her sunken eyes, Helle told me what everyone in *Laager* had been saying about my mother and Onu Gusti: "They do it in the WC."

"Do what?" I asked.

"You know...." Helle drawled, and then she gave her little secret smirk, similar to Onu Gusti's, now that I think of it.

Whenever the women spoke about certain things, children were told to leave the room. We were not supposed to hear about the atrocities of war either, but this was different. The timbre of their voices was higher, not so serious. It would be accompanied by a sly sort of smile, like Helle's and Onu Gusti's. Sometimes there would be a smattering of laughter, either raucous and loud or muted and giggly. Everyone else seemed to know something that completely escaped me. Even Annie-Mannie knew more about such things than I.

During that summer Ema took me swimming along with some of her women friends in a nearby river. I didn't have a bathing suit, but she said it was okay to go in the water wearing just my underpants because I didn't have any breasts yet and there were no men around. She was never opposed to nudity as long as it was just among women. But I was shy about my nakedness and stayed in the water, too embarrassed to come out wearing only underpants. Until I saw a funny-looking fish, oblong and transparent.

"Look at this!" I shouted, holding it aloft for my mother to see. "A jellyfish!"

Ema stood up then and beckoned me out of the water.

I covered my bare chest with one hand and carried the fish in the other.

The women tried to hide their laughter by turning their heads or placing their hands over their mouths.

"*Pfui*, Tita!" Ema exclaimed. "Throw that away immediately. Don't you ever touch one of those filthy things again."

"Why?" I asked. "Is it poisonous?"

More titters. Even Ema was trying not to smile.

"It's filth," she said. "It's for sex."

I felt as though I was floating on a body of water that contained secret depths. Something took place in the dark under the bedclothes that everyone knew about but of which I was totally unaware.

Men are interested in only one thing, Ema had repeated often enough, but she never elaborated on what that might be. I was desperate to find out the truth, yet there were questions I could never ask my mother.

Finally I decided to approach Proua Nelli, a large, boisterous woman who talked so freely about everything that whenever she came around, children were immediately shooed outside to play. She knew fortune telling and laid out cards for everyone in the block. This was an important private business among the ladies that they indulged in almost as often as playing bridge or double solitaire.

One afternoon when Ema was still making tea in the kitchen, Pr. Nelli arrived before any of the other women. I took advantage of the opportunity.

"How are babies made, Proua Nelli?" I asked as timidly as possible, and, though my heart was fiercely thumping, I tried to give her my sweetest smile. "I know that a man and a woman have to touch," I added, to indicate I wasn't totally ignorant of such matters and didn't expect to hear some hokey blabber about storks and such.

Pr. Nelli didn't disappoint. "They don't just touch, honey," she shouted out cheerfully in her jolly deep voice. "He sticks his big thingy right into her." Then she laughed, *Ha-Ha-Ha*, as if this was the biggest joke in the world.

I was horrified. Surely not that huge purple swollen ugly protrusion that Annie-Mannie and I came upon when our mothers were sunbathing nude in the bomb hole? Was Onu Gusti truly concealing one of those monstrosities underneath his brown gabardine trousers, smiling his phoney smile while waiting for the opportunity to stick it into my mother? In the WC? like Helle said. And what would happen if Ema did indeed have a baby? She would surely prefer the new child to me.

It was obvious that I must become even more watchful. Onu Gusti wouldn't dare try anything while I stood as witness. I'd tattle on him for sure. To my father, the next time he came to visit. Or to his own wife even, if I ever happened to see her again.

17.
Isa

ISA STILL WROTE TO ME, but not as often. He came to visit a few times, bringing his clothes for my mother to mend. He hung around during the day, but he always spent the night someplace else. Ema was still angry about the dog, I could tell. They didn't exactly fight, for she hardly talked to him, though she looked less than happy to be sewing on his buttons. None of us ever mentioned Kati. The silence that Ema had forged between us made me feel awkward with my father.

He had promised to take me on a trip during the summer, just the two of us, so we could get to know each other better. I wasn't looking forward to that. Once we were alone, he might question me, and I was never supposed to mention Onu Gusti.

What I could hardly wait for was summer camp. The Scouts and Guides were spending the whole month of July by a large lake near the Austrian border. We younger ones were going to be there for one week.

Our tent was already set up for us when we arrived. Our leader, one of the older Guides, assigned us the job of decorating the front area with whatever we could find in the woods to represent our troop of eight girls. We worked all afternoon. The cool, fresh breeze from the Alps and the surrounding forest recalled a magical time and place that I had almost forgotten among the cement pavements and stone buildings of Hochfeld *Laager*. We constructed an Estonian flag from blue flowers, black twigs, and white pebbles.

"You girls did a real nice job," the leader commended us and sent us down to the lake to wash the dirt off our hands. We then lined up at the outdoor kitchen with our tin plates for the stew that the older campers had spent the afternoon preparing. At sundown, wearing our light blue neckerchiefs, we marched in formation to ceremonially lower the Estonian flag and sing the national anthem. The remainder of the evening was spent around a huge campfire, listening to ghost stories, singing, and searching for constellations among thousands of stars in the black sky. In the tent, two to a cot, it was hard to settle down. There was a lot of suppressed giggling and a burst of great hilarity as one girl fell out of bed, rolling through the canvas edge right into the woods. Seemingly no more than a few moments had elapsed before a trumpet sounded the reveille. Shivering in our pyjamas, we were herded once more to the lake to brush our teeth and wash our faces in the cold water.

At breakfast, the camp leader gave us some very bad news. A sixteen-year-old Guide named Juuli had become ill some days before our arrival and had been taken to the hospital. It had now been confirmed that she had polio, which caused paralysis and could be deadly. It was also very contagious. Camp was over. We never even got to swim in the lake. Buses arrived to take everyone back to Augsburg, and directly to the hospital, where we were placed in quarantine for two weeks.

What at first felt like a supreme disappointment turned out to be a lot of fun. Almost like camp, in fact, except for the swimming and the hiking and the stars. We played games, did all sorts of crafts, and had pretend campfires at night where each group put on an entertainment. As no parents were allowed to visit, a crowd of them gathered underneath the hospital windows every evening after supper to wave and to throw kisses. Right away I spotted Ema and threw kisses with both hands until I realized she was not alone. Beside her stood Onu Gusti. I felt my face harden into a sullen pout. They must have planned this all along. They could do whatever they pleased while I was away at camp unable to keep my eye on them. They were glad I was stuck here in the hospital for fourteen days. They'd be even happier if I was gone forever. It would serve my mother right if I got polio. Then she'd be sorry.

But no one else came down with it.

Ema wasn't waiting outside the next evening, nor did she ever come to wave to me again. I didn't care about her anyway. I was having too much fun. In fact, I hardly thought about her at all. When we were released from the hospital, she told me that she and Onu Gusti had taken a trip. She showed me some pictures of herself in front of a castle, on a bridge, standing by a lake. She was wearing a new flowered dress of a flimsy material I had never seen before, her long brown hair blowing in the wind. She was smiling into the camera, smiling at Onu Gusti.

I sulked for several weeks thereafter and told her it was because I was disappointed about camp. She tried to cheer me up by bringing home the funny papers from work to read to me in the evenings, and she also taught me to play double solitaire. Still, it took me a long while to forgive her.

A few weeks before school began again, Isa came to take me on our adventure as he had promised. I didn't want to go as it would give Ema another chance to be with Onu Gusti on her own. Also I was sort of scared, not of my father exactly, but because I had never in my life been alone with him before. Would he be disappointed in me? Would he be strict? Would he ignore me altogether? Once we got under way, however, all my worries ceased, and I felt a freedom in my own being that I had never experienced before.

Isa paid far more attention to me than my mother ever did, but noticed me less. He never told me what to do or complained that I was not behaving correctly. I could tell that he liked me, that he was enjoying this trip as much as I was. He let me steer his old car, sitting on his lap, speeding along the *Autobahn*. We sang *Krambambuli* at the top of our voices. We went swimming in a public pool. He held me under the tummy so I could kick my legs and move my arms, and I was never afraid that he would let me go. He took me to a sauna with him and asked me to beat his back as hard as I could with a bundle of birch boughs. He gave me a sip of his wine. We stopped to visit his friends in various *Laagers* across the breadth of Germany, and he introduced me as his beautiful little daughter. *And this young lady I've brought here with me is my beautiful little daughter*, he would announce and then wait, looking down at me as if he expected applause.

I loved my father, and so did everyone else.

Men would come over to greet him, slapping him on the shoulder, pumping his hand all the while.

Women liked him also. He was tall and handsome. He had a car. He was kind to his little daughter, charming, irresistible.

Whenever a woman spoke to him in a certain way, I became jealous and went off by myself with a book, but it wouldn't take long before he came to look for me.

Aha, here you are, Tots. What's that you're reading? It must be a very exciting book for you to be here all by yourself.

He listened attentively to everything I said and always made me feel important and interesting. I was a soldier's daughter, a brave little Estonian girl whom he loved with all his heart, and it would make everyone so happy, especially him, if, when I finished that page, I would come back and join the party because everyone missed me.

Our last stop was in Geislingen.

Proua Tamm answered the door. She looked the same as I remembered, with her light brown hair and startled eyes.

"Volli? This is a surprise!" she cried. "Gus isn't here," she added. As she glanced down at me, her smile faded, and I had a sudden vision of where he might be. Nevertheless, she invited us in, offering coffee and biscuits.

"Children, look who has come to visit!" she called. "It's the little girl you played with when we lived in Dresden."

Marika and Enn looked different. More grown up. I could tell they knew very well who I was, but pretended not to. I was proud to be there with Isa. *See,* I felt like saying, *I have a father too, and he's far more handsome than yours!*

"Why don't you take your guest to your room and show her your toys and books while I talk a bit with her father? Pr. Tamm instructed.

Obediently, Marika took my hand and led me to the children's bedroom. Their place was huge compared to our tiny room in Hochfeld *Laager*. They had the whole bottom floor of an entire house, and a garden besides.

I had just shouted out *BINGO* very loudly when Pr. Tamm entered with a stern look on her face. Was I too noisy, perhaps?

In *Laager,* children were often warned to be quiet because other people lived there too, but she just beckoned to me with her finger.

"Come with me," she said, "I have something I want to show you."

Some papers were clutched in her hand. She took me into the WC and closed the door. Then she grabbed me hard by the shoulder.

"Look, child," she whispered, shoving the papers at me. They were letters. I recognized my mother's handwriting. "Your mother wrote these to my husband. Look at what she says. Here, read. You can read, can't you?" She was very upset. Her face was swollen with despair and fury, her hands shaking.

I pretended to look, but I was too frightened to read. The words spun in front of my eyes.

"Here," Pr. Tamm hissed, grabbing the letters from me. "Here, look here. See this lipstick mark? It's a kiss she is sending to him. Your mother is a wicked woman. She should be ashamed of herself!"

Both of us were crying now.

My father must have heard us, for he knocked and then opened the door. "We better go now, Tots," he said softly, taking me by the hand.

Back in the car, he dried my tears with his handkerchief and made me blow my nose. "Don't pay any attention to her," he said. "Those are just the ravings of an unfortunate woman."

He didn't seem at all upset about the incident and tried to cheer me up with songs and funny stories all the way back to Augsburg. I was sad to say goodbye. He promised to come again soon and that we would be best pals forever.

I didn't mention anything to my mother about going to Geislingen.

18.
Estrangement

JUULI REMAINED IN THE hospital for the rest of the summer. School was already in session when she came back. She looked very skinny, and she was in a wheelchair. Because of the polio she wouldn't be able to walk ever again for the rest of her life. We all felt sorry for her. We made cards and wrote poems, and even cried a little.

There were so many things happening that fall, I hardly had time to miss my father. It was nice having a room to ourselves once again, this time on the third floor. Not only that—the couple across the hall had a small dog, Pitsu. He had sharp ears, a stubby tail, long whiskers, curly grey fur, and I adored him. *Don't you dare give any of your food to that dog, Tita,* my mother warned, but Pitsu spent a lot of time under the kitchen table and was especially fond of the gristly meat Ema made a great show of saving just for me.

Proua Maas, our English teacher, gave me a letter from the United States. She lived with her family in New York, the girl wrote. Not in the city, but in the state. She was the oldest child. She was in Grade Four. Her teacher had told them about poor starving DP children who had lost everything. She liked to write letters and wanted a pen pal in a foreign country. *Please write back*, she wrote. She included a glossy coloured photograph of three beautiful little girls in red coats and straw hats with the word ME and an arrow pointing to the biggest one. I soaked the stamp off the envelope and added it to my collection. Pr. Maas helped me write a reply in English.

One day, Ema came home from work wearing her angry look.

I was busy with my homework, and couldn't remember having done anything wrong, but she accosted me even before taking off her coat.

"Tita," she said, "why didn't you tell me that your father took you to Onu Gusti's house?" Immediately I felt the flush of guilt race up to the roots of my hair.

"I don't know," I said.

"Why don't you ever tell the truth?" she shouted in exasperation. "Why can't you be open and honest with your mother?"

I looked down at my notebook, my lower lip drooping.

"Tell me," she demanded, lifting my chin sharply with her clawed finger.

"We went to visit all sorts of people," I said. "Isa said it might be nice for me to see Marika and Enn, since we were friends in Dresden." Ema looked at me sternly to see if I was telling the truth before letting go my chin.

"And then what happened?" she asked.

"Nothing. We played a game. Bingo."

"Did Proua Tamm say anything to you?"

"She showed me some letters."

"Did you read these letters?"

"No," I said. "But I saw them. She said you wrote them to Onu Gusti. She showed me a red lipstick mark. She said you were sending him kisses." I felt justified. It was Ema who was bad, not me. "She said he was *her* husband and that you were a wicked woman."

Ema said nothing for a while, and I gloried in my triumph. But not for long.

"Oh, you foolish child," she finally began. "And you believed her? Where is your loyalty to your mother? I did write to Onu Gusti, yes. We are good friends. He saved us from the Communists. He offered to buy me some lipstick. The red mark was where I indicated the colour I wanted."

We never spoke about it thereafter, but I knew something was going on. Proua Nelli came often to lay out cards for my mother. They whispered grown-up talk that I was not allowed to hear. Some yellow roses arrived. They were from Onu Gusti. But he never came to visit us again.

Isa came though, as he had promised, and Ema was even meaner to him than before. We went into the kitchen and sat at the table while she warmed up some barley soup, slammed down three bowls and three spoons, and brought over the pot. We ate in silence, my father nodding his head appreciatively as though he hadn't eaten for weeks. I kept the pout on my face, more out of fear than anything else, scared I might say something to start them off, or maybe call him Onu by mistake.

At night when I pretended to be asleep, I heard them arguing.

"You give us nothing," Ema said. "You spend all your money on yourself and on the women. How dare you come here with the smell of chocolate on your breath when you never bring your child anything."

"You always were cold as ice," he told her. "Why does the child call me 'Onu?'"

I must have fallen asleep then, for the next thing I knew it was morning. Her black coat was gone from the closet but Isa was still sleeping, his long lean body splayed over the narrow bed.

When I got home from school that afternoon, I expected him to be gone and was surprised to see his car parked in front of our building. I took the steps two at a time.

He was sitting on the bed with his jacket on, his arms on his knees, his head sunk into his hands. The bedclothes were askew and heavy with the sour smell of sleep. The words I came in with remained in my mouth.

"I've been waiting for you, Tots," he said softly. He patted the bed for me to sit next to him. "I've been waiting for you, my dear little daughter," he repeated, "to say good-bye forever. Your mother won't let me come to see you anymore."

"Why?" I gasped. "Why not?"

He didn't answer, just put his hands over his eyes. I could tell he was crying. Because of me. Because he couldn't come to see me anymore. After some time, he pulled his fingers down hard over his face, sighed loudly, kissed the top of my head, picked up his suitcase, and went out the door. Through the cheesecloth curtains, I watched him drive away.

The room was almost dark when my mother returned from work. By then I had stopped weeping, but my face remained hot and swollen, my nose stuffed up. I felt like I did when I had a fever.

"What's happened? What's wrong?" Ema called out, alarmed, tossing her coat on the bed, feeling my brow with her cool hand. "Are you sick, child? What hurts?"

I began to cry once again. Great heaving breaths shook my body. I was ashamed to tell her. I knew she wouldn't like it.

"Isa said he would never be able to see me again," I sobbed. "That you wouldn't let him."

She soothed me with cold cloths. She took me into her lap and rocked me. She warmed a cup of milk and stirred in a spoonful of our precious honey to sweeten it. Gently she scratched my back with her long hard fingernails. Then she began to defend herself.

"I know you love him more than me," she began. "All he has to do is show up once in a while and entertain you. And he's good at that. Always has been. I have to feed you and clothe you and bring you up right. He gives us nothing. He spends his money on his women and himself. He puts the last bit of chocolate into his own mouth and then walks up the stairs to kiss his little girl. He expects me to take care of you on my own and to feed him and sew the buttons back on his shirt when he comes. He thinks it's the way it should be because I am still his wife. But I refuse to do this any longer. If he doesn't provide his share, he cannot see you. That's true. I will not permit it. I told him that. It's his decision. He always was a good faker, although you, child, don't understand that. Weeping his crocodile tears to gain sympathy, to get one more chance, to get his own way. Making a dramatic exit. He's a charmer. He's charmed you, I can see that. But he'll never take care of you. I'm the only one you have, and you better get used to it."

She got up briskly from the bed then, hung up her coat, straightened the unmade bed, and went into the kitchen to prepare our dinner.

I felt I had no choice except to purge my father from my heart.

19.
Departure

A RUMOUR WAS CIRCULATING in *Laager* that many countries would soon accept DPs as immigrants. Belgium and England had already opened their borders. Canada, Australia, and Argentina were to follow. The United States was still holding out, it was said, but not for long. Everyone was eager for a new life in a better place. People were applying for immigration, and the gates of our future life were about to open.

One girl from my class had already left for England. Her mother was going to work as a nanny for a rich family. Others were planning to sign up as farm labourers in Australia. The world to which we had become accustomed was disintegrating once again. Helle told me that her mother had a relative in Canada and that they might be moving to a city called Toronto. Most Estonians wanted to go to Canada because it seemed more civilized, more like Europe. But it was not simply a matter of choice. The immigration process was long and arduous, rife with bureaucratic hurdles. Before anything else, one had to find a sponsor—either a company or an individual willing to provide a job and to guarantee that the DP would become a productive and useful citizen.

Although my mother's first choice was Canada, she had a friend, Marta, with an aunt in the United States. We referred to her as the "Old Estonian," because she had been living there for many years. This woman devoted a great deal of time and effort attempting to find sponsors for Estonian DPs. She travelled all over New England, Marta said, doing her best to promote us to church groups, to businesses, to individuals, to anyone who would listen and might sign an affidavit saying they would guarantee an Estonian DP a job. Marta urged my mother to send a letter to this woman right away, listing her qualifications and attaching our picture.

Young people, couples without children, and families with fathers had a much greater chance of being accepted as immigrants. Annie-Mannie's family and some others had applied to go to Seabrook, New Jersey to work at a corporate farm that grew and processed vegetables. Both Aldo's and Mari's families also had connections in the United States. The Astis were heading for Australia. Single mothers had a harder time finding sponsors, and those with more than one child were in despair as no one wanted them. Ema was trusting in her guardian angel, she said, but also hoping that Marta's aunt might be of help.

Wearing our best—me in my national costume and Ema in her wool dress (the one with the tufts of brown yarn to cover the moth-holes that she made in Austria)—we posed for a photographer. Surely someone would take pity upon this attractive looking young mother and her charming little daughter and sponsor us as immigrants. I was almost ten by then and in my fourth year in school. Although life continued on pretty much as always, there was a pervasive restlessness in the air. People were leaving, and no one knew who would be saying goodbye next.

My pen pal from New York State sent me a book of four paper dolls. On the front and back covers were two sets of big and little sisters, blonde and brunette, so modern that they could be punched out instead of cut with scissors. The inside of the book was filled with beautiful clothes for all of them, printed on shiny paper. I let Helle and even Annie-Mannie cut out some of the outfits. We tried them on the dolls, but after that we didn't know what else to do with them. They were much too fine to associate with the maimed inhabitants in my Hochfeld tenement book, and home-drawn clothes looked stupid on them. Ema said it was time to start getting rid of old things anyway since we would soon be leaving *Laager* to begin a new life across the great ocean in a different country. I performed a little ceremony before burning my tenement dolls in the stove, including Princess Elizabeth and Prince Philip wearing their wedding outfits. I also threw in the fashion dolls that various older girls had drawn for me along with all the clothes I had made for them—there was no way these could compare with the glossy printed ones from *Ameerika*.

A few days before Christmas, the last one we spent in *Laager*, I was shocked to see Isa's car parked in front of our block. Although we still wrote to each other, I now regarded this as an obligation. I belonged to my mother. She was the one who took care of me. We had only each other. There was no one else. I didn't want my heart to be torn apart. I never wanted to see my father again. But there was no question of running away or even delaying my entrance; I was supposed to come home right after school and do my homework. As Ema didn't return from work until a few hours later, I had to face him alone. Slowly, stopping to put two feet on each step, I ascended the three flights of stairs and opened our door. Isa was sitting on my bed with a big smile on his face. The room was filled with presents wrapped in bright paper. Next to him rested a wooden sled with a big red bow tied to the runner.

"Hello," I said, but didn't run into his outstretched arms as I used to.

His smile faded then, and his eyes hardened. He could tell I no longer cared, that I belonged to Ema. He didn't call me over to sit on his knee or throw me up into the air shouting *KRAM-BIM-BAM-BAMBULI*. I sat across from him on my mother's bed in my dark woollen stockings and school clothes, prissy and alone. We made small talk like strangers, cold and distant, about how much I'd grown and what I was learning in Grade Four. Finally he indicated the presents, the sled.

"These are for you," he said. "Don't you know that?"

"For me?" I gasped, pretending surprise, feeling awkward and foolish. I knew he brought them only because Ema warned him that if he ever came again he had better bring me something. Like both my parents, I had the stubborn Estonian pride bred right into me: *If you feel obliged, don't bother*. But of course I didn't say that out loud.

"Who did you think they were for?" he asked me seriously, in a quiet voice. I could tell he saw right through the pretence and didn't like me as much as he used to.

It was a relief when my mother came home. She sat beside me on my bed, and I clung to her. Isa left soon after and I didn't care. It was too hard to be a good child to two parents who hated each other. It wasn't that easy to be good enough even for one.

In the New Year, we got word that we might be going to the United States. The "Old Estonian" had found a family—the Johannsens—who agreed to sponsor us. Marta told us in a letter that they were proprietors of a chicken farm in Rhode Island. The husband had a Swedish background and the wife was Finnish, so they were sympathetic to the plight of the Balts. They liked our picture and wanted to help unfortunate people in need. They had two young children themselves, a son and a daughter about the same age as me. If we passed government inspection, we would be going by ship over the Atlantic Ocean to live in *Ameerika*.

We had a month to get ready. Ema purchased a sturdy wooden chest to hold the possessions we would bring with us. On the top, she painted her name and our new address in big bold letters: FOSTER CENTER, RHODE ISLAND, U.S.A. I had to discard everything that would be of no importance in our future life: my schoolbooks and scribblers, my red ball and lucky hopscotch stone, my pick-up sticks and marbles, my bottle of purple ink, the paper dolls from my pen pal. I doled out my treasures to those children remaining on our block who had not yet found sponsors: my doll, my new sled, my roller skates, most of my clothes, even my national costume. I would soon grow out of it anyway, Ema said. Besides my clothing, I was allowed to take my stamp collection and three of my favourite books. We were going to a new land, dragging with us a few personal belongings, plus the old useless values and customs we were afraid to discard, for without them we would have nothing at all.

Ema made me a new winter coat for the trip and knitted a hat of Estonian design with a scarf and mittens to match. She also made me a warm woollen dress that I wore for my passport picture. For herself she made nothing. She would enter *Ameerika* in her threadbare black belted coat with a green babushka covering her hair.

We were on the threshold of an unforeseeable existence.

She was able to procure a book about chicken farming, and every night she practised her high school English out loud: *Hello. How are you? I am fine. I cannot yet speak English very well. Please, where is the* WC? *Dank you very much.*

Isa came to see us off. He brought someone with him who was much prettier than my mother: a beautiful, sophisticated-looking woman wearing a sheared fur coat. She was an Estonian actress from Geislingen. Of course I was jealous. I hated her. And I hated him. It made our parting easier. He kissed me goodbye, but neither of us cried.

As I look back at my life in *Laager*, I don't think I could have been happier anywhere else. I enjoyed school. I liked piano lessons and folk dancing and Sunday school. I was a young Guide (*Hellake*), and I wore my blue uniform and light blue neckerchief to meetings. I sang in the children's choir. I had a starring role in a play. I made some mistakes, but I had a lot of friends. It was the only time in my life that I had no doubt I belonged within a group of people just by being who I was.

The continuity of inheritance that provides a shield from the transitory nature of life was no longer an option for us. I wish I still had those paper dolls I threw into the stove, and my pick-up sticks, and the beautiful white rocking horse left behind in Estonia, and the national costume Ema sewed for me with such exacting stitches. I wish I could look at them now, and pass them on to my children. But a handful of pictures and the book my father made for my sixth birthday, written in a language no one in my present world understands, are the only mementos that remain of my childhood.

After World War II, billions of dollars were spent to aid the refugees in Europe. The relief agencies were there to efficiently implement distribution. Within a relatively short time, the majority had been resettled, and by the early fifties most DP camps were disbanded. It was a commendable success story—except for the 250,000 leftovers not accepted for immigration (the old, the infirm, the crippled or otherwise disabled, the single mothers with too many children who could not get sponsorship). Still, even this unwanted refuse was eventually taken in by various European countries on a humanitarian basis. The rest were assimilated into German society. In 1957, the last remaining DP camp was shut down.

PART III
IMMIGRANTS

20.
Resettlement

PRIOR TO BOARDING THE SHIP that would take us across the Atlantic Ocean, we were sequestered at the Resettlement Centre in Bremen. Ema and I were the only Estonians among a throng of emigrants from *Laagers* all across Western Germany—Poles, Ukrainians, Latvians, Lithuanians, Yugoslavians, Czechoslovakians, and a number of Jews who managed to survive ethnic cleansing and were now DPs like the rest of us. The administrators spoke English, but our common language was German.

Like everyone else, my mother was being evaluated as a commodity, with me as a part of her baggage. Since the United States government was paying the cost of our passage, several weeks were spent ascertaining whether she truly had the potential to become a productive member of American society. At the Resettlement Center, we were poked and prodded, disinfected, deloused, injected, inoculated, and thoroughly inspected from top to bottom. It was discovered that I was nearly blind in my right eye, for I could hardly make out the top letter on the standardized chart. The doctor said it was congenital but Ema blamed it on too much reading in bad light. I was fitted with a pair of round dark-rimmed glasses, one lens as thick as a magnifying glass, making the inferior eye appear immense.

"You have to wear them all the time, Tita, or your eyes will get even worse," Ema warned. "That's what the doctor says."

Putting a thick piece of glass in front of the deficient eye made no difference to my vision whatsoever. Didn't they realize I had always seen the world as it appeared to me? Whatever depth perception I needed, I invented myself. I took the glasses off whenever Ema wasn't around to scold me. They made me look ugly, worse than I felt already, stupid and dumb, since, during our time in *Laager*, and speaking only Estonian, I'd forgotten most of the German I used to know. There were some other kids my age at the Center, but when I tried to talk to them, I sounded like a two year old. So I kept to myself.

  The Resettlement Center made an attempt to acclimate us to our new life. Classes in deportment and language were offered. Ema discovered that the table manners she had taken great pains to teach me—knife in the right hand, fork in the left—were useless. In *Ameerika*, after cutting a piece of meat, you had to switch the fork to your right hand before putting it into your mouth for it was impolite to use the left hand for eating. This took a lot of practice and some patience, especially when you were hungry. To indicate you were finished with your meal, both utensils were to be laid side by side on the edge of your plate, the knife on the outside. Vegetables, fruits, and soft gooey pastries were cut with a fork, never a knife. Rolls and bread were torn apart with the fingers before being buttered. The butter knife was used to transfer a pad of butter to your plate, never for spreading. Certain forks were for salad or for dessert, depending not only on their size but also their position in the place setting. Some foods, such as carrot sticks, drum sticks, and celery, were to be picked up with the fingers, same as bread, cookies, small pastries, and candy. A chocolate bar, for example, was never eaten with a knife and fork. Neither was a frankfurter ("hot dog") or a *kotlett* ("hamburger"). These were enclosed in oblong or round buns and eaten like a sandwich—a hot dog was held in one hand, while for a hamburger you used both.

  Instead of keeping your hands on the table at all times, which was mannerly in Estonian circles (*Where are your hands, Tita?*), they were to remain in one's lap to secure a piece of thin paper, the napkin, so it wouldn't fall onto the floor for it would be very awkward to crawl under the table to retrieve it. The napkin was employed to occasionally wipe the corners of one's mouth and to be left beside the plate when the meal was over, unfolded but never mutilated. *(Don't shred it into bits like that, Tita.)*

A piece of pie, with the point facing you, was always eaten with a fork, not a spoon.

A bigger spoon was used for soup, a smaller one for puddings and ice cream or to stir tea and coffee.

The only time it was acceptable to tuck a napkin into your collar like a bib was to eat a lobster (something I never saw in actual practice until fifteen years later).

It was hard for a ten-year-old to remember it all. Only a few things remained the same: don't talk with your mouth full, don't chew with your mouth open, and never slurp the liquids.

Ema heard that in *Ameerika* even older women were referred to as *girls* or sometimes *gals*, and people who weren't relatives or close friends might call you by your given name, which astounded her. Also, that it was impolite to say *What?* Rather, one should always say, *I beg your pardon?* She said it often, first because she didn't understand what people were saying to her and later because her hearing deteriorated. I do believe it is the only thing she ever begged for in her entire life.

Finally, with all our papers and medical forms reviewed and signed, our pictures taken (me in my new dress, my mother in the old one she had made in Landeck), our passports were stamped and Ema and I were both officially approved for immigration to the United States of America.

We left Bremerhaven, Germany, in March, 1949, on an old troopship, the *General Black*, which heretofore had been used to transport American soldiers. The new immigrants were each assigned a bed in two enormous rooms solidly crammed with row upon row of bunks—the men on the lowest level, the women and children on the floor above. This departure was not at all similar to when we left Estonia. No one stood on deck singing the national anthem until the land faded from sight or took along a handful of German soil to remind us of what we were leaving behind. We were glad to go. We looked forward to a new life full of infinite possibility.

Due to my insistent nagging, Ema initially allowed me to sleep in the top bunk, though the bottom one was safer. We ate our meals in a large dining hall in shifts, with an endless supply of apples and oranges always available as snacks. Shy at first, I soon met a few other girls my age, getting along quite well with the bit of German each of us could muster, playing card games that everyone knew no matter what the language. An older Ukrainian girl drew paper dolls for us. We were allowed out on the upper deck during the day. After we passed through the English Channel and into the open ocean, the ship began to sway in the swells and we had fun pretending to be drunk.

Ema brought some Estonian newspapers with her. In the evenings, we lay side by side on her bunk as she read them out loud to me. I started a diary, but soon lost interest and it got thrown out.

The seas were high. Many people were seasick. On the fifth day, we encountered a fierce storm. It was impossible to walk without holding on to something stationary. Ema switched bunks with me, fearing I might roll out of bed. We were both nauseous and throwing up. The latrines were disgusting. The stench of vomit and engine oil and oranges permeated everything. No one was allowed out on deck. A few ancient looking men wearing life vests sat on the steps, praying to Jehovah for protection.

"They just want to make sure they're the first ones to get out into the lifeboats," Ema sniffed. "A big ship like *General Black* will never sink," she reassured me.

And she was right, for after ten days on the ocean, we landed safely in the port of New York. Some passengers, seasick for the entire duration of the crossing, had to be helped from the boat; a few were carried off on stretchers. I was lucky. I only threw up for three days. Ema was sick for longer.

We were exhausted and wobbly. The ground swayed beneath our feet. Large white tags were tied to our coats to identify us with our names and numbers. We looked like all the other DPs in the newsreels of the time, *The Eyes and Ears of the World*, which for many years were shown before the main feature in the movie theatres. A pale, bewildered herd. Some elderly ladies passed around donuts and hot chocolate to the children. We were in *Ameerika*. I expected it to look a lot different, but it seemed much like any other place.

Crowded together in a large dingy room, we waited for our

baggage to be unloaded. After some hours, my mother's name was called on the loudspeaker. A wonderful surprise awaited her: Someone had come to meet us! Our sponsor, Mr. Johannsen, had driven all the way from Rhode Island to pick us up. A tall, large-featured man with enormous hands, his feet encased in sturdy boots, helped my mother carry our big chest of possessions outside and shoved it and our suitcases into the trunk of his big shiny car. It was of a maroon colour with velvety seats, a lot fancier than Isa's or Onu Gusti's.

We drove through the immense, tall, grey city of New York for a long while before the landscape became woodsier. Mr. Johannsen asked if we were hungry, and though we politely shook our heads, he pulled off the highway anyway and stopped at a place called the Five and Ten. We sat at a counter on red stools that spun around though I wasn't allowed to and he treated us to what he called a real American lunch—a hot dog with mustard and relish followed by a piece of apple pie. I didn't like either one, but I said "dank you very much" and "I like," and remembered to hold the hot dog in my right hand and turn the tip of the pie toward me before I broke off a small piece with my fork. Mr. Johannsen smiled and patted my head with his huge red hand.

It was nearly dark when we arrived at the chicken farm in Rhode Island. Mrs. Johannsen greeted us with egg sandwiches on white bread and glasses of milk. Their two children, Ingrid and Frank, whom the Johannsens called *kids,* were both younger than I. They stared out of big blue eyes as if looking at something they had never seen before in their lives. Perhaps they expected us to appear like we did in our photograph—me in my national costume and Ema in her best tweed dress. What we really looked like must have been disappointing. We could hardly speak English. I was wearing my new round glasses. We staggered a bit when we walked because we had been on the ocean for so long, and we probably still stank from the vile fumes of *General Black*.

The next day was Sunday. "We will spend this day to get to know each other," Mrs. Johannsen said. "On Monday a school bus will come to take the kids to school." She spoke to us in a very loud voice as if we couldn't hear well in addition to being impaired in all sorts of other ways.

Again we start anew. We are treated gently and examined cautiously, wounded birds brought inside a human habitation. The kind-hearted folks want to help, but don't know quite what to do. They repeat soothing words. They offer food. They smile to indicate that their intentions are good, and we try to respond in an appreciative manner, although we exist in two distinct realities, worlds apart.

We were shown our room. A double bed had been made up for us with clean, sweet- smelling sheets, two folded towels with matching washcloths placed on top.

"This is good?"

"Jaa. Guut. Dank you very much."

"Good night, then."

"Guut night. Dank you very much."

The room swayed around us, but we were in the United States at last. In Foster Center, Rhode Island, at the Johannsens' chicken farm. On Monday, I would be going to a new school where everyone spoke only English. I understood a little, but could not yet speak. They would assume I was stupid.

"Well Totsu," my mother said, "we are here! We made it! We are going to be chicken farmers in Ameerika!"

She sounded happy. Even as a child, I was never as positive in my outlook. On Monday I would be on my own.

21.
Foster Center

IN FOSTER CENTER, we were already celebrities. Newspaper people came the next morning to interview us and to take pictures. Mrs. Johannsen did most of the talking. Ema nodded her head a lot, saying *guut, guut, jaa, jaa*. They posed us for a photograph: Mrs. Johannsen holding a drumstick, my mouth open for a bite. It already smelled delicious. After the picture was taken, I hoped she would let me eat it, but she put it back into the oven.

When the reporters left, we sat down in the dining room for our first meal together. They called it Sunday dinner: Roast chicken, mashed potatoes, buttered peas and carrots, chocolate pudding with whipped cream for dessert. My mother was right: Hands are kept under the table, and even the kids shift the fork from the left hand to the right after they cut their meat. I tried to remember everything we had practised, nervously shredding my napkin into disgraceful bits, a humiliating pile of residue I eventually had to disclose for all to see.

The photograph, along with the story of our arrival, appeared in the local paper the following day. *A grateful DP child is given food by her American sponsor,* said the caption underneath the picture. I looked so ugly in my new glasses with my mouth wide open, almost drooling, that no one could be blamed for thinking they allowed an idiot to come to *Ameerika*. Nevertheless an envelope addressed to me arrived in the mailbox. It contained a card depicting a picture of a four-leaf-clover saying "Good Luck," and was signed *From a Friend*. Inside was a dollar bill.

"Our first money! And you earned it, Totsu!" Ema exclaimed.

The Johannsen chicken farm was not anything like the farm in Estonia where Memme and I stayed when I was little. There were no hayfields or berry bushes, no dogs or cats, no flies crawling on the windowpanes. There was no barn with cows to milk and pigs to feed or horses to pull wagons. I didn't even see hens or roosters or baby chicks. The birds were all locked up in a huge, long, red building way out in back that we were never invited to tour.

There was no job for Ema at the chicken farm either. They were not rich, Mrs. Johannsen said. She was very sorry, but they couldn't afford to pay any wages, though we were welcome to stay and Ema could help around the house until she found employment somewhere else.

My mother tried to keep a cheery countenance and said *Jaa, jaa,* but I could tell she was disappointed.

"I have a dollar," I reminded her.

She didn't say anything, just ruffled my hair as Onu Gusti used to.

When they were first shown our photograph, Mrs. Johannsen explained, they felt so sorry for us that they agreed to be our sponsors. They had been assured by the Estonian woman who came that DPs are hardworking people, capable of finding jobs easily anywhere in the United States. What was important, the woman said, was to give these poor refugees a chance to lead normal lives again. For that, all she needed was their signatures on a piece of paper. And here you are!

School in *Ameerika* was hardly what I expected either.

Monday morning, after a breakfast of Corn Flakes covered with milk and sprinkled with sugar, Ingrid, Frank, and I went outside to wait by the mailbox. We each carried a brown paper bag with the lunch their mother had prepared for us—peanut butter and jelly sandwiches, carrot sticks, a hard-boiled egg, and an oatmeal cookie. Shortly, a dark blue car with a sign stuck on the roof that said SCHOOL BUS slowed down and pulled over. We clambered into the back seat. The bus also picked up an older boy further down the road who sat in front with the driver. After what seemed to me a considerable distance, we stopped at a small white building with FOSTER CENTER ELEMENTARY SCHOOL painted in big black letters above the door.

The school consisted of one large room. We hung our jackets on hooks in the back and placed our lunch bags on the shelf above. There were eight desks of various heights, each with a chair attached, and a much larger one by the blackboard. Behind this, a very stout woman was sitting—the teacher. She got up to greet me and hugged me to her flowery bosom with her fat arms. Her name was Mrs. Frytags, she said, but it was okay for me to call her Mrs. Eff. I found out later at recess that everyone actually called her Old Frybags whenever she was not around to hear.

Mrs. Eff led me to a medium sized desk and motioned for me to sit down, checking to be sure my knees fit underneath properly and that my feet reached the floor. She gave me a brand-new pencil and showed me how to sharpen it in a small machine in the back of the room. The toilet, which she pointed out to me from the window, was in the little hut out back. After these preliminaries, she tapped on her desk with a long wooden ruler, a *yardstick*, as a signal that we were all to stand for the singing of the American national anthem that was sung in Germany whenever officials attended *Laager* ceremonies. *Ou sei kän ju sii*—I begin, but I didn't know the rest. After this we placed our right hands on our chests where our heart was supposed to be, turned to face a flag of thirteen red stripes and forty-eight white stars that dangled from a pole in the corner, and everyone (except me) recited some words. Then we got busy. Mrs. Eff handed each of us a sheet of tan paper and pointed with her yardstick to the math equations covering the blackboard.

"Do all the ones you can," she said to the class.

Mathematics overcomes all languages. By this time I had learned to add, subtract, multiply, and divide. I finished all the problems easily and was the first one done. When I showed her my work, Mrs. Eff pressed her lips together and nodded her head many times, her big chins wobbling.

"Aha!" she said, peering at me from small shrewd eyes encased in crinkly layers of fat. "This is very good, young lady. Now, how about your reading?"

She handed me a book about Dick and Jane and assigned a partner to help me. Starting over once again. Back at zero.

SEE DICK.

SEE JANE.
SEE SPOT.
SEE SPOT RUN.

Brightly coloured pictures depicting how children lived in *Ameerika* took up most of each page. Dick and Jane wear nice clean clothes, play with their dog Spot, sell lemonade to friendly neighbours passing by on the street for two cents a glass, and often carry big balloons. I could hardly wait to become an *Ameerikan* myself.

At noontime one of the older boys delivered a small glass bottle of milk to each of us from the refrigerator by the door. After we ate our lunch, we went outside. The students in this school might possibly say nasty things in a whisper behind one's back, but they were much too bashful to be mean to one's face. I did catch them staring, though. They played *Tag* and *Steal the Stick*—games known to children the world over—and motioned for me to join them. After a while Mrs. Eff stepped outside, ringing a bell to indicate recess was over.

When we went back in, we pushed aside the desks to practise a dance.

Four couples formed a square. Since there were eight of us now, I took Mrs. Eff's place as the partner of the biggest boy. He was thirteen. He hardly glanced at me and refused to take my hand, holding on to my sweater-sleeve instead with his thumb and index finger. This was a rehearsal for some sort of performance—I understood that much—and no one seemed happy about it. The dance was very easy: Three steps in, three back, circle around, change your partner, and do the same all over again. The manoeuvres we were taught in the Estonian folk dancing troupe in *Laager* were many times more complicated.

That night, the "Old Estonian" who found our sponsors drove to the farm to meet us. Her real name was Proua Unger, and she spoke Estonian the way my mother spoke English, apologizing for having forgotten so many words because she left Estonia as a very young girl after the First World War. Up to that point in my life I had always thought there was just the one war—our war. Why would people do anything so horrible more than once? I still have not found a satisfactory answer to that question.

Pr. Unger looked wealthy. She had wavy white hair and wore lipstick, earrings, and a fancy coat with a fur collar. She was aware all along that our arrangement at the Johannsens' would be temporary, she said, but she didn't want to scare Ema unnecessarily before we got here. In America there were plenty of jobs for anyone who was willing to work, she continued on in her halting Estonian, searching for the right words. Advertisements appeared in newspapers every day. She knew someone who was willing to help. He had already assisted some other DPs, and she was sure he wouldn't mind driving Ema around to find her a suitable position and a place to live.

"Welcome to the United States," Pr. Unger said in English, hugging both of us. "It's a wonderful country. You will do well here, you'll see."

All of her life, Ema believed that a guardian angel sat on her shoulder watching over her. This time the angel manifested itself in the form of Mr. Hooey, a gum-chewing, heavy-set, bald-headed man wearing a pale blue cap with a peak in front, who drove a black pickup truck and smelled strongly of garlic. He took a long, hard look at my mother. Right away I became suspicious, but Ema seemed grateful. She told him she didn't care what kind of position she got as long as it wasn't as a servant in someone else's household or a public washroom attendant. Anything else she was willing to try.

While I was at school, Ema rode around in Mr. Hooey's truck looking for a job. It only took her a few days to find one. We were going to move to a different state altogether, she told me, to the town of Essex in a place called Connecticut.

On the Friday night before we left, we attended the spring concert at the Consolidated High School, where my class was to perform the dance we had practised all week. This school was huge compared to Foster Center Elementary with lots of classrooms and a parking lot full of cars. We entered a large, noisy auditorium. Parents and guests sat in the back; the performers were assigned rows in the front. Mrs. Eff greeted us in an unfamiliar dress—an enormous green field sprouting pink flowers. The students looked different also—the girls in lace and taffeta; the boys with their skinny heads poking out of starched white shirt collars and wearing neckties. I gaped around at all the other kids. They seemed much more confident, livelier, louder, more the way I expected *Ameerikans* to be.

A written program was handed out at the door. *Folk Dance— Foster Center Elementary,* was scheduled near the end. We watched funny skits and listened to singing groups. A long line of rabbits danced "The Bunny Hop" through the aisles, finally ending up on stage to take a bow.

I had always enjoyed performing in my previous life but a terrible shyness overcame me now. Rehearsing for the final time that same afternoon, our dance didn't seem too bad. Now I realized that it was altogether ridiculous, stupid and hokey compared to the other acts we had been seeing. But nothing could be done as Mrs. Eff bustled our group onto the stage and there we were, fixed in our square formation, the three little ones, the three bigger girls, and the tall gawky fellow in his white dress-shirt, his face bright red with embarrassment. Even before the music started, there were a few titters from the audience. I knew they were laughing at me, the DP, a foreigner, in my round-rimmed glasses and wearing my best woollen dress that Ema sewed for my passport picture, not at all like the others.

When Mrs. Eff put on the record and signalled us to begin our dance, one of the little kids remains staring out at the audience, forgetting to move. My partner makes an ugly face about holding my hand. Frank Johannsen stumbles in his big shined-up shoes. Someone gets mixed up and starts going the wrong way. The laughter was quite loud by this time. Perhaps if I hadn't come and taken Mrs. Eff's place, she would have kept the dancers in line. But then again, it may have provoked even more hilarity. After we finished, I heard someone holler *BOO!*

They were ridiculing not only the DP, but all of us. It was clearly obvious that even if born in the United States one can still be looked upon as a hick, a rube, a geek, a moron, a dummy, a retard—words I didn't learn until much later. I made a vow right then and there that I would never end up as one of those.

Thus began my long and arduous struggle to be an American.

The morning after the performance, Mr. Hooey came to take

us away. My mother had found a job in a place called the Soda Shoppe. We would be boarding with a family who had a daughter a bit older than me. Mr. Johannsen and Mr. Hooey hauled our suitcases and the big trunk into the back of the truck while Mrs. Johannsen and Ema hugged goodbye, both of them wiping away tears.

22.
Essex

IN ESSEX, WE OCCUPIED one of the upstairs rooms of the Bentons' three-bedroom, two-storey white clapboard house at the edge of town.

As to why they took us in, I can only speculate. Surely not because they needed the extra money. What Ema paid for room and board couldn't have been more than a pittance as her salary was ten dollars a week plus tips. Perhaps the Bentons were friends with the proprietors of the Soda Shoppe, doing them a favour by providing accommodations for the new employee. Maybe they were interested in having a companion for their only daughter, Amanda, to widen her cultural perspective as people do nowadays by sponsoring foreign students. Or it could be that they were being kind to a woman in need, a single mother recently arrived from Europe, a DP with a job in the village and no place to live.

I remember the Bentons clearly:

Mr. Benton: Small, energetic, round-faced, with dark wavy hair, rectangular unframed glasses and a ready smile, wearing a wristwatch with a leather band and favouring crisply starched, well-pressed, short-sleeved white shirts.

His wife: Nearly as tall but much thinner, her frizzy light brown hair hanging to her shoulders. I don't know what he did at his job, but she spent her days in brightly-printed, freshly-laundered housedresses committed to a well-defined schedule of household tasks.

Their daughter, Amanda: A chubby girl of twelve with dark naturally curly hair and nasty things to say about almost everyone she knew. At first, she was quite excited to have a real DP child to order around, but after she got to know me better, she got tired of it. I didn't like her very much either.

Mr. Hooey delivered us and our belongings to the Benton household on Easter weekend.

The Easter Bunny of my previous existence strode upright upon long, furry, brown legs, wore a blue jacket and carried a large wicker rucksack on his back filled with beautifully coloured eggs which he left on the doorsteps of good little boys and girls. In *Laager*, Ema decorated hard-boiled eggs while I was asleep and hid them in a bowl filled with fresh green moss to surprise me in the morning.

At the Bentons', Amanda and I each received an enormous basket encased in bright yellow cellophane.

"Look what the Easter Bunny left for you two girls!" Mrs. Benton exclaimed, clapping her hands together.

I pretended surprise and clapped also, but Amanda merely scoffed. The baskets were filled to the brim with sweets—chocolate rabbits, marshmallow chicks, jelly beans of many colours, big bright sugar-coated eggs and smaller ones wrapped in shiny gold and silver. Because it had never been necessary before, I had learned no restraint in regard to food. *Finish everything on your plate,* was the rule. By evening all the candies in my basket were gone.

I knew, of course, that the Bentons had provided the treats. I was almost ten-and-a-half, and I didn't believe in any of the lies children were told. I even had serious doubts about some of the things Ema believed in, like her guardian angel, which Isa had labeled superstitious nonsense.

It must be acknowledged, however, that Ema's guardian angel had been keeping a watchful eye on me as well. If we had arrived in Essex right away instead of Foster Center, I would certainly have been placed in a much lower grade in this larger, more modern school. Because I didn't speak English, I might have started in Grade One all over again, growing breasts and towering over my classmates like Tamara in *Laager*. But in the one-room schoolhouse at Foster Center, with only eight pupils of such varying abilities, the skills I did have were noticed.

To each according to his need and from each according to his ability, was the educational philosophy of the kindly and wise Mrs. Frybags. When I left her classroom only five days after I had arrived, I was already beginning to understand most of what was said to me, was the best in the school in mathematics, and could read out loud from the Grade One Dick and Jane books. Due to the letter evaluating my achievement that Mrs. Eff wrote, I was placed in Grade Five. The decision may also have been influenced by the fortunate circumstance of Amanda being in in the same room, as the class happened to be a Grade Five/Six split.

During the remainder of that year in Essex Elementary School, nothing was asked of me and nothing was expected. I spent most of the remaining two months of the school year in the back of the room, at the easel painting pictures or at the small loom weaving mats. Quiet and undemanding, I was easily forgotten. When we moved again in the beginning of the next school year, my records indicated I was to enter Grade Six. In this manner, instead of being held back, I skipped an entire year, remaining the youngest in my class from that time on, barely seventeen when I started university.

One of my mother's favourite stories about our early days in the United States dealt with her first job at the Soda Shoppe. She fully expected to be washing dishes in the kitchen and was astounded when they fitted her with a uniform and put her behind the counter.

"I do not know how to speak English very well," Ema protested, but they assured her she would do fine.

Not only did she have to improve her English—and fast—but she had never before heard of sundaes, milk-shakes, ice-cream cones, sodas, BLTs, and French fries, these staples of American cuisine being as foreign to her as the Estonian treats of bloodwurst and headcheese would be to the people she served. Slim and quite fetching still in her little waitress cap with her continental accent and willingness to please, she became a big hit right away. We were a novelty, the only DPs in that well-to-do small seaside town. Customers were patient and eager to help. She was tossed into the ocean without knowing how to swim, but as there were people all around to keep her afloat, she learned quickly.

She worked six days a week, lunch and dinner, with a three-hour break in between, and had Sundays off. On Sunday afternoons we walked the five blocks to the town centre to attend the matinee at the local movie theatre. Every Monday morning, a new poster would appear on the big billboard outside advertising the next weekend's movie. I could hardly wait, especially for the ones in Technicolor and the musicals—*Paleface* with Bob Hope and *A Connecticut Yankee in King Arthur's Court* with Bing Crosby. A concession stand in the lobby sold candy bars and boxes of white puffy stuff called popcorn. When my treats were gone, I'd start on my fingernails.

Stop that, Tita! Ema would whisper.

But I couldn't stop, and neither her beautifully manicured hands nor her constant nagging could deter me. After the nails were done for, I'd start on the cuticles. *Orally fixated*, I found out later in Introductory Psychology; the opposite of my mother who was definitely *anally retentive*.

On Saturdays, Amanda and I were allowed to go to the town centre by ourselves. First we poked around in the Five and Ten, where one could buy all sorts of remarkable items for less than a dollar. I spent my money on a book of paper dolls. This was not a wise purchase, for after I began to cut them out I realized they weren't nearly as nice as those my pen pal had sent to me in *Laager*. I was getting too old to play with dolls anyway. It must have been a lapse of judgment due to a momentary nostalgia. Full of regret and shame, I didn't tell my mother that from my dollar I had only nine cents left.

During these excursions, we would stop at the Soda Shoppe to sit on the high stools along the counter. My mother, in a brown uniform and white apron with a brown-and-white striped cap on top of her head, would treat us both to an ice cream cone. Later, Amanda would meet her boyfriend down by the waterfront while I waited for her on a park bench. She made me promise not to tell.

One hot afternoon in late spring when we arrived back home, we climbed up into the shady fork of the large maple tree in the front yard to sit and rest. There Amanda revealed her secrets. "We kiss a lot, but we haven't done anything yet," she said.

Even though my English had improved considerably, I had no idea what she meant.

"What do you say in your language," Amanda demanded, "when a man and a woman do it?"

"Do what?" I repeated stupidly.

"You know," she said with that same little smirk I had come to recognize whenever the subject came up, "make babies?"

Helle had told me a word. I didn't know if it was the right one or if she just pretended to know to show off, but I passed it on.

"Nick," I said.

"Nick?" Amanda laughed. "There's a boy in our school named Nick."

We both giggled.

"In America we say 'fuck,'" she told me. "My mother and father FUCKED and got me."

That too seemed totally hilarious.

Not to be outdone, I said, "My mother and father NICKED and got me." And then, even more boldly, "My mother and Onu Gusti NICKED but got nothing."

We couldn't stop laughing at that until suddenly I noticed a dark shadow directly under our tree. It was Ema, on her break, returning from work. She had been standing there for some time, listening to everything we said.

"Tita! Get down here immediately," she commanded in Estonian, grabbing me by the back of the neck and marching me to our room.

I was one of those children who never had to be spanked. I felt so terrible whenever I did something wrong, I'd be bawling long before punishment was even mentioned. The willow switch my mother kept on top of the closet in *Laager* was never taken down. Its mere presence was enough.

"I'm sorry, I'm sorry," I whined. "Amanda asked me and I told her."

"I'm truly ashamed of you, Tita," Ema scolded. "How could you say something so filthy about your own mother? I'm the only one you have, and you have only me. We are here together in this foreign land. You have hurt me very, very much."

Then she left, shutting the door of our room, and went downstairs to inform Amanda's parents of what she had overheard.

I hardly remembered what we had actually said, except for the bad word in two languages, but felt awful nevertheless. How could I have hurt my mother like that? All of a sudden, a horrible thought presented itself—what if Ema decided to hang herself because I was such an evil child? What would happen to me then? I lay down on the bed sobbing loudly until I fell asleep. *High-strung*, my mother often called me. *You always were a high-strung child.*

The next morning my face was still splotchy and puffy, my eyes red and swollen.

"Did your mother beat you?" Amanda asked.

"No," I said. "Did yours?"

Amanda seemed surprised.

"Why would she? We didn't DO anything. We were just talking. Mom and Dad thought it was funny."

I was too young to understand about reaction and overreaction, over-protectiveness and repression. All I knew was that sex was filthy. It was bad to talk about and to think about, and especially bad to actually do it. Unless you were married. And then it had to be done. *We got married and then we had you.* But what about Onu Gusti? Did he do it with his wife and Ema both? I wondered, immediately ashamed that such an evil thought could ever enter my consciousness.

The next dirty word I learned was five years later, when I was a sophomore in high school. My best girlfriend told it to me. The word was *FART*.

23.
Discovering America

AT FIRST HAVING ME AROUND was to Amanda's advantage. As a DP child who had experienced the war first hand, I received a lot of attention that rubbed off on her also. But it didn't take long for her to arrive at a different conclusion. I could hardly speak English, I wore ugly round glasses and homemade clothes, I acted like a baby a lot of the time, I was not interested in boys, and I was getting chubby from all the candy I so compulsively consumed. Not only that—my mother was a waitress, a profession just a notch above cleaning woman. Soon Amanda made it obvious that she no longer wanted to associate with me unless she absolutely had to. I didn't really mind. She was sort of fat herself and not nearly as popular as the girls she admired.

There seemed to be a birthday party for one or another of these girls nearly every week, and those who invited Amanda were obliged to invite me also. We would play games like Pin the Tail on the Donkey, eat enormous slabs of frosted cake topped with huge mounds of ice cream, watch a pile of presents being opened, and then go home with a party favour, which usually included a container full of candies.

In America, sweets abounded. My mother brought home innumerable boxes of chocolates given to her by customers: *Here's something for your little girl, and save a few for yourself, doll.* If she weren't protected by the counter, they might have added a quick pinch as well, I reflected later. *That's the way men are,* I can hear her saying. Mr. Hooey also brought chocolates whenever he came to see how we were getting on, which seemed to be quite often. It was no wonder my teeth rotted and my clothes became tight around the middle.

During our time in Essex, I did make one friend on my own. Her name was Mary. Her mother died when she was just a baby. She was in our class at school and lived with her father a few houses down the street from the Bentons, but she was never invited to any of the birthday parties. She had red hair, a face covered in freckles and, though she was only twelve, acted like a grown-up. She cleaned the house, cooked supper for her father, and babysat for a relative to earn spending money. Amanda said she was very homely, but I didn't care. Sometimes Mary invited me to her house to play board games like checkers or Monopoly. I admired her greatly, even though my personal goal was to be more like Tessie or Wendy or Connie or Sally or Susie—those rich girls with the beautiful clothes who lived on the other side of town in huge fancy houses, had birthday parties, and were always laughing and happy.

After a while Mary's real purpose for spending time with me manifested itself: she wanted to fix up her father with my mother. She even invited us to come to dinner one evening so they could meet. But Ema wasn't the least bit interested in men. Not Mr. Hooey, not Mary's father, not Mr. Benton, nor any of the customers at the Soda Shoppe who gave her boxes of candy. She had lost Onu Gusti, the love of her life. She didn't want another, and I was glad.

In June I received a letter from my old pen pal at our new address:

> *I am so happy that you have come to America. We live just outside of New York City, not very far from Essex. My mother says I can invite you to stay with us for a whole month when school is over so that we can all get to know each other. She will come to pick you up. My mother is going to write a letter to your mother. I hope you can come. It will be a lot of fun.*
>
> *Love, Your pen pal*

Ema gave this invitation some serious thought. We hadn't been apart from one another since we left Estonia, except during my quarantine in the hospital and the road trip with Isa. In this new country, she was determined to keep a particularly watchful eye on me. But as she now regarded Amanda a bad influence, especially during school vacation when we would be spending much more time together, she allowed me to go.

The Maxwells were exactly what I expected Americans to be. They resided in a large white house among others of similar size, all surrounded by tall leafy trees and set back from the street by well-tended green lawns. The back yard, with flowers growing all around the edge, contained a flagstone patio with a built-in barbecue, a swing set and a slide, and a small building for gardening tools. There was a circular paved driveway in front and an attached two-car garage.

Every weekday morning, Mr. Maxwell, dressed in a blue suit with a grey tie or in a grey suit with a red patterned one, drove one of the cars to the railroad station to take a commuter train to New York City. On weekends he stayed home wearing khaki pants and a polo shirt. The other car belonged to Mrs. Maxwell. She had blonde wavy hair and wore red lipstick. She smiled a lot and was very active, always going here or there, wearing denim skirts and comfortable shoes around the house, but high heels and a fancier outfit when she took us places.

There was a grumpy, white-haired grandfather who had his own private suite in the basement and spent most of his days in front of a little box, the TV, watching cowboy movies.

There was a big rust-coloured dog named Rusty.

A maid came daily to clean the house and prepare lunch and sometimes dinner, but she looked just like a regular person and didn't wear a uniform.

The three Maxwell daughters were princesses, the same as in the picture I stared at with such rapt attention when we still lived in *Laager*. Beautiful. Tiny and lithe, their golden curls cascading over their shoulders, flitting about in their fine clothes, whining and nagging and complaining and fighting but pampered just the same.

The Maxwells were prepared to introduce their America to this cute little DP girl who posed so prettily in her national costume in the picture they received along with the letter written in English that they all chuckled over. She had so recently arrived with her mother, so destitute, so poor, so in need of some love and attention.

But I was not what they expected.

Behind my round glasses my eyelids felt puffy with unshed tears, my lips were sullen, my fingers bit raw. My mind was tormented by things I didn't understand. Everyone thought me stupid, and I was stupid. Also clumsy. And awkward. And ashamed of being so fat and ugly and miserable. Paralyzed by shyness, I sought solitude. I would rather hide in some dark corner chewing my nails than expose myself to ridicule. The Maxwell girls were sprites, and I was the ugly gnome they tried their best to entertain. I didn't know how to be like them, my feet solidly stuck to the ground, dumb as a stone. I was repulsed by the bloody barbecued meat, barely charred on the outside that they served for dinner. I wasn't taught in the Resettlement Center that one should eat corn on the cob neatly row by row and took messy random bites. I was not interested in the tiny blurred black-and-white images on their new TV, preferring books so I could create my own much more vivid pictures. I was lonesome for the Estonian language and the ways of my mother. I wrote to her every day. These people, the Maxwells, remained strangers to me, and I was aware that I must have been a disappointment to them, saying *dank you very much* with no real understanding of what I was supposed to appreciate in a world that had nothing to do with me.

During the week, *we girls* as Mrs. Maxwell called us, spent our days going on excursions—to the Bronx Zoo, to Coney Island, to the top of the Empire State Building, to Radio City Music Hall, where a long line of Rockettes kicked up their legs in perfect unison. On the Fourth of July, we watched the fireworks from the deck of a sailboat anchored in Long Island Sound. Loud noises terrified me. I covered my ears and hid my face while everyone else cheered as yet another volley of explosives whistled up into the black sky.

The Maxwells belonged to an exclusive private yacht club. On weekends, members were ferried to a small island, with a restaurant, tennis courts, changing rooms, and a playground for the children. It was only years later, while occupying a miniscule space at Jones Beach among thousands of others, that I truly apprehended their affluence.

The Maxwell girls were eager to get to the Club. Immediately upon arrival, we all ran to the small cubicles that served as changing rooms to put on our bathing suits. They had been told to wait for me so they could introduce me to their friends at the beach.

"Come on! Hurry up"! they shouted, but there was no way I could force myself to open the door to face them and their friends. In the dim security of this private space I chewed my fingers and pressed myself against the rough wooden wall.

"Let's go!" I heard someone say. "She'll find us."

I waited for what seemed like a very long time before I dared open the door and peek out. Everyone was gone. But as I cautiously emerged, one of the friends spotted me.

"There she is!" he shouted, pointing a finger. "She's coming out. She's a great big girl," I heard him laugh. "I thought she'd be a little baby."

They were all crowded together at the lower end of the beach and I felt too humiliated to join them. Not that day, nor the next, and not even the following weekend when they knew enough to leave me alone. I shied away to the other side of the island where the adults swam, walking out until the water was up to my chin and no one could see me. Grasping the rope enclosing the swimming area, I practised what Isa had taught me long ago, kicking my legs gently below the surface of the water. Soon I was able to hold on with only one hand. When I let go completely, I discovered I could float. Each time I went out a bit further, keeping close to the rope but no longer hanging on. In this way I taught myself to swim.

At the end of the visit, the Maxwells brought my mother down for our last weekend together. Leaving us children in the care of the crotchety old grandfather, the grown-ups went out for cocktails and dinner and to the theatre. Hopefully, Ema redeemed me and made these kind people feel good about their efforts on our behalf. She was truly grateful. She said it had been a long time since she had felt like a human being, like when she was young, like she had been before the war.

I wrote a thank-you note to my pen pal, but didn't get a letter back and we never saw the Maxwells again. Mr. Maxwell was transferred to California shortly after our visit. A few years later, Mrs. Maxwell died of cancer. He then started to drink too much. Eventually he lost his job, and the Maxwell girls were no longer wealthy. That's what Ema told me, for she kept track of almost everyone she ever met through hundreds of annual Christmas cards. Except for the Bentons, strangely enough. Something must have happened while I was away. After we moved from Essex, she never mentioned them again.

24.
Servitude

WHEN I RETURNED from my visit, everything seemed different. Amanda and I got along far better than we used to. My English had improved due to four weeks of not speaking any Estonian, and she was impressed by what I had to report about my stay with the Maxwells. I didn't lie, but I was beginning to discern what not to reveal. I told her that we took an elevator to the very top of the Empire State Building, saw a spectacular show at Radio City Music Hall, and went to Coney Island (leaving out that I was afraid to go on any of the rides except the merry-go-round). I also mentioned that the Maxwells had a TV, two fancy cars, and a sailboat, and that they belonged to a private yacht club on an island where we went swimming every weekend. Amanda was very aware of social distinctions, so I advanced considerably in her esteem.

My mother and the Bentons hardly saw each other. Ema remained in our room during her break, resting, and ate her meals at the Soda Shoppe. Mr. Hooey came on her day off to take us on various excursions around Connecticut. Though he always brought me chocolates, I placed him in the category of the slimy sort of men I abhorred. My mother didn't like him much either, but he did have a truck and was willing to drive her around. He introduced us to a family of Old Estonians and some recent immigrants like us, who lived in Hartford.

One hot Sunday morning at the end of August, after much haggling, Ema allowed me to go to the beach with the Bentons instead of being dragged along with her and Mr. Hooey. Waterlogged and scorched by the sun, we were eating a light supper of bologna and cheese sandwiches in the kitchen when Ema returned to make her announcement.

"We will be moving next weekend. I have found a new job."

The Bentons seemed to expect this, but I was shocked. We were just beginning to settle in. I was looking forward to starting the school year along with everyone else, no longer as *the new kid*. How could she do this to me?

"Why?" I asked when we were alone in our room. "Why do we have to move? I like it here." Because of her work hours, she said.

"At my new job, we will be together all the time, Totsu," she added with a smile.

Amanda and I cried real tears at our parting and promised fervently to write. She did send me one letter saying her parents were getting a divorce and that she and her mother were moving to Florida, but that's the last I heard.

I suspect Ema wasn't telling me everything. Something must have happened while I was away. Or perhaps she had come to realize during her time with the Maxwells that working as a waitress and sleeping in the Bentons' spare room wasn't what she wanted from life. It is not just one thing that determines the course of one's history. She may have been looking for a new job all summer. Whenever I asked her later about why we left Essex so suddenly, she would either claim it was so long ago she couldn't remember or give the same old story about wanting to keep a closer eye on me, which her hours at the Soda Shoppe didn't allow. Forthcoming in her opinions, Ema never talked about her personal life. Yet she always insisted I tell her everything. Because she was my mother, she said, it was her right to know.

During one of my annual visits many years later, I came across a large yellowed envelope I had never seen before even though we had lived in such proximity to one another. Inside, carefully preserved between folded sheets of thin tissue paper, were two photos of the face I had so despised, inscribed: *To my darling Emps, With love, Gusti, Dresden, 1945.* I did know that he lived with his family in New York City and had resumed his career as a successful architect, but I was still reluctant, even embarrassed, to ever mention anything about the role August Tamm had played in our lives. Not wanting to hurt her or to provoke her anger, I kept my memories of Onu Gusti to myself as our guilty secret. Ema may never have realized how deeply the events of my early childhood were imprinted into my being. How could she? Only once, in my late teens, during a heated argument in which I felt unjustly accused, did I spit out the words:

"I remember you having an affair with a man married to someone else."

She winced but recoiled quickly.

"That was during the war," she replied. "Everything was different then. You know nothing about it, Tita."

Ema's new job was at a prestigious preparatory school for boys. She had been hired by Dr. and Mrs. Prout, the headmaster and his wife, to take care of their six-month-old baby. Not as an actual servant, she made sure to emphasize, but as a nanny with only light housekeeping duties. Although circumstances sometimes dismember the most vehemently held opinions, it truly surprised me even then that she had elected to work as a domestic, something she vowed she never would do.

"We are moving to a magical place, Totsu," she enthused as we packed our belongings into the Foster Center chest yet again. "We'll be living in a mansion that looks like an enchanted castle in a storybook, surrounded by deep, dark woods. And Baby Lil is a little princess. You'll see."

In Essex, we had been displayed upon a game board of tidy white houses and green lawns, tip-tapping our way down Main Street like a couple of wooden tokens, stopping to pay our dues at the Soda Shoppe, the Five and Ten, the Cinema, while real life took place in the unfathomable space around us. At the prep school, Ema and I became the hidden ones, concealed within the castle, watching royalty file by in their golden opulence. Holed up in a dark attic room at the Headmaster's Residence, we were summoned only when required. And a ten-and-a-half-year-old DP girl was not needed by anyone at all.

Who is that?
No one.

Even Ema, busy from morning till night with Baby Lil and

household duties, had little time left for the sullen, painfully shy, downward-looking child sulking in a corner, picking her nose in secret, chewing her nails in public. Totsu vanished and Tita took her place, huddling behind the fancy panelled wooden wall of the headmaster's dining room which concealed a dim stairwell leading to the servants' quarters, her fingers in her mouth, her lank blonde hair damp with perspiration. How many hours had she been sitting here? There was company for dinner. Ema was serving. She listened to the blunt clank of silverware on fine china, the murmur of elegant conversation interspersed with bursts of laughter, waiting for the voices to cease, for the chairs to scrape back from the table, so she could open the secret door and sneak down into the kitchen to be with her mother, too terrified to climb up the dark curving staircase into their room with its small-paned reflecting windows and unfamiliar shadows. There were people close by, on the other side of this door. The murmur of human voices beyond the wall had cushioned her fear.

Now there was only silence.

She remained still for a moment longer to make sure that dinner was truly finished and everyone had left. But when she pushed on the door she found it was bolted shut from the other side. She was locked in, not allowed to intrude into the privileged realm of the rich no matter how desperate she felt. Yet upon reflection, perhaps it wasn't such a good idea to infringe upon her mother in the kitchen. Ema would most certainly be displeased.

You are no longer a baby, Tita, she would say. *You are almost eleven. Go back to our room immediately. There is nothing to be afraid of here.*

Resting her cheek on the hard, oaken step, she tried to keep herself awake, alert for her mother's footsteps. Before the bolt was drawn, she must scuttle up the stairs to quickly compose herself in her bed, pretending to be asleep.

One day when no one else was around and Ema was busy feeding Baby Lil in the kitchen, she dared to explore the rest of the castle, using a small door which connected the servant quarters to the rest of the house. She was as edgy as a thief, ready to bolt if she heard anyone coming. First she looked around upstairs. The private places. The master bedroom with a double bed and a bathroom off to the side. The headmaster's study, containing a desk and bookshelves. Two other bedrooms adjoined by a bathroom, for guests, and a nursery painted pink and filled with stuffed animals, books, and toys. But she was too nervous to linger anywhere for long. Just long enough to imprint it all in her mind, before noiselessly descending a staircase of large rectangular stones that led to the foyer below. The enormous living room was down two more steps to the left: Ceiling-high bookcases filled with leather-bound volumes she was not allowed to read; a grand piano she was not allowed to play; opulent velvet sofas and chairs she was not allowed to sit upon, for it would leave a mark. On the other side of the hallway, a guest suite containing an immense canopied bed covered in maroon brocade. Further on, the dining room with its massive table and high-backed chairs where she was not allowed to eat. The walls were hand-stencilled with a blue-and-brown pattern, except for the one panelled in dark oak which was cleverly designed to conceal a door leading up to the servants' quarters. She alone knew that on many nights behind this door there was a child, almost eleven. Pressed into a corner of the curving staircase, chewing her nails, hoping that if someone attacked her, or if there was a fire, or if she dared to scream loudly enough, a rich person might hear and open the door that was bolted from the other side. None of that ever happened, of course. The scream remained imprisoned, dutifully guarded by the servant's daughter who was not allowed to make any noise.

A long corridor, lined with glass-fronted cupboards containing a collection of exquisite antique china, led from the dining room into the kitchen, where Ema spent the greater part of her days and where the servants ate. Also Baby Lil. There was another servant, a tall, stooped, gentle-voiced black man named Sam who lived elsewhere, not on campus. Sam was supposed to do all the cleaning; Ema was hired to look after the baby, to prepare and serve breakfast, and occasionally, only if there were special guests, also dinner, for the headmaster and his wife usually ate their main meals in the Refectory among the faculty and students. As is often the way of immigrants, Ema strove hard to do a good job to prove her worth, gradually taking over more and more of the duties that were supposed to be Sam's. Sam worked slowly, and it took him an hour to do a task that Ema could do in ten minutes. Not too long after we arrived, Sam was fired and my mother became the sole servant in the household.

The headmaster's name was Dr. Paul O. Prout. Because of his initials, the students called him "Dr. POP, Sir," even to his face. He was short and stout, a man of formidable energy, wit, and artistic talent, impatient and demanding. Mrs. POP was far more approachable, though her eyes tended to wander away from you after she asked you a question and her joviality seemed overdone. Later I came to realize that what she presented to us was her public persona.

Both Prouts were very pleased with the new nanny and said so. It had been difficult in the past to find household servants and even harder to get dependable men for the menial jobs in the school kitchen and on the grounds. The pay was low, the hours were long, the housing inadequate—a dormitory of dingy rooms in the basement of the Power House. Mostly the work was seasonal, only while school was in session. Many of the workers were derelicts, drunks, or drifters,

"There are still Estonians in the DP camps in Germany who are looking for sponsors," Ema informed Dr. POP.

He would be very happy to hire more DPs, he said. And thus Dr. POP became a sponsor.

The school was situated in a large acreage of forest and accommodated about two hundred and fifty wealthy boys from grades seven to twelve. It was a community onto itself, as faculty and staff lived on campus also. I took the bus to attend public school in the nearest town, three miles away.

Due to our move and settling in, I missed the first couple of weeks of the school year, once again to be introduced by the teacher as *our new student and I expect all of you to make her feel welcome.* There was a bit of tittering, and someone laughed out loud when she said my name, wrote it on the blackboard, and identified me as an Estonian. By now, although many people in the United States had heard about DPs, hardly anyone knew of Estonia. A few kids tried to be helpful, most ignored me, some made fun of me. By this time I was able to read better than the lowest group of "slow learners," but I still knew nothing about what wasn't taught in the classroom. How to hit a softball, for example. I attacked the ball as one would swat a fly and would always strike out. No one wanted me on their team. It was hard to make friends when you despised yourself, so I turned to books once again.

In November, Grade Six put on a play for the rest of the school entitled "The First Thanksgiving," which told the story of a thirteen-year old Czechoslovakian DP whose family recently immigrated to America. Although no one there was aware of my previous acting experience and great success as *Jänku Jukku, the Rabbit* in the Hochfeld *Laager* production, the teacher picked me for the starring role. I had no problem memorizing the lines and spoke them loudly in a convincing foreign accent. A few days later, a picture of me appeared on the front page of *The Hartford Times*, suitably dumpy in my hand-knit Estonian sweater and ugly glasses, as if I'm wearing a costume to play the part. Also a short article with the headline: A REAL DP PLAYING A DP.

That same afternoon a flurry of activity ensued at the castle. I was hurried to the telephone by Mrs. POP herself. A call for me from the secretary at the Governor's office in the State Capitol. The Governor's daughter, Sally, apparently saw my picture in the paper and remembered me from her fifth grade class in Essex before they moved to the Governor's Mansion in Hartford. The Governor would like me to come for a visit. The secretary then asked to speak to my mother to confirm the invitation. After that, Mrs. POP got on the phone to ascertain the arrangements.

A few days later, a long, black limousine arrived at the front entrance of the exclusive private school to pick up the servant's daughter. The boys gawked from dormitory windows. Mrs. POP, my mother, and Baby Lil all waved as I was driven away. It resembled a scene from a musical, I thought proudly, with me as the star.

At the Governor's Mansion, Sally greeted me and we were treated to ice cream and cake. Although we weren't really friends, I remembered her from the birthday parties I attended in Essex. The Governor himself, a large bald-headed man, visibly sweating in a three-piece suit, also stopped by to say hello. No pictures were taken, but there was another telephone call for me a day later, causing a second small stir in the Prout household. A reporter from the newspaper wanted to interview me about the visit. How did I feel about being invited to the Governor's Mansion? "Very good, dank you very much." When he asked what I wanted to be when I grow up, I answered, "A movie star." Ema told me I was stupid to say that.

We had been in America for less than a year, and I was already famous. My picture and several stories about me had appeared in the newspaper. A limousine driven by a chauffeur had transported me to the Governor's Mansion. I was interviewed by a reporter who called me on the telephone. All sorts of people must know who I was by now. When my mother had a day off, we got a drive to the village centre and took the bus to Hartford to walk around the big department stores and check the sale racks in the bargain basements. I expected people would recognize me right away, but no one appeared to. In the afternoon, we went to the movies to watch a musical in Technicolor, *Annie Get Your Gun,* with Betty Hutton and Howard Keel, which served to reinforce my career ambition even if Ema did disapprove.

They might someday make a film about a young girl, a DP who comes to America and ends up as a famous movie star, I mused as I lay awake in bed that night. The film would end with a close-up of my face, tears streaming from my eyes as I sang "God Bless America." I switched on the light and got up to practise in front of the mirror, trying to achieve a starry look. I even managed to bring forth some tears.

25.
The First Christmas

AT THE END OF DECEMBER, the Prouts took Baby Lil to Baltimore to spend the holidays with her grandparents. They wished us a fine Christmas and told us to make ourselves at home. For five days, the castle was ours.

Although by then I realized that where we had our living quarters was merely the well-appointed Headmaster's Residence in a posh private school, for the first time since our arrival I could walk around freely. I longed to steep myself in the delights of Baby Lil's nursery: the closet hung with beautiful frocks, the cupboards crammed with toys, the shelves lined with books, but the family quarters upstairs still remained forbidden territory.

The Prouts' dachshund, Fritz, left in our care, followed me wherever I went. I taught him to roll over, to give his paw, to sit up and beg. Fritz and I tried out all the velvet chairs, loveseats, and sofas in the parlour. I attempted to read a few of the leather-bound volumes from the wall-to-wall bookshelves, but they were filled with words I did not yet understand. I opened the lid of the huge grand piano and played "Für Elise" on the sparkling ivory keys, pressing down the mute pedal so the sound wouldn't carry to alert my mother, careful to wipe off any fingerprints on the mahogany with the hem of my skirt. Next, I took off my shoes to jump on the huge canopied bed in the guest suite, raising a lot of dust but smoothing down the red brocade cover when I was done. No longer apprehensive of the small windows and the dark recesses, I pretended I belonged here, that I was in disguise and my real name was Princess Lil.

Due to Ema's persistence and Dr. POP's sponsorship, there

were now four other Estonian immigrants living at the school, all newly arrived from DP camps in Germany: broad-faced Nelli, servant to the Dean; grey-haired Joosep, who washed dishes in the Refectory; and Peeter and Eerik, doing maintenance work on the grounds. All of them seemed old to me in their fusty clothes with their servile manners, even though Eerik was still in his twenties. They never talked about what used to be. Who they were and what they did in Estonia was no longer of any importance. They must have had families, but they were alone now. Our personal histories had become extinct. The only thing left was our common language and traditions. None of them spoke English. My mother was the interpreter.

Nelli occupied a small attic room in the Dean's residence, similar to ours. The men were quartered with other menials in the basement of the Power House, sleeping in compartments separated by thin unpainted plywood panels, each space just big enough to accommodate a single bed and a metal locker. There were no windows. The floors were cement. A communal area was equipped with a card table and a few folding chairs. A faded green-toned backseat ripped out of an old sedan served as a sofa. A wooden radio sat on a shelf in the corner. Several square glass ashtrays overflowed with stale butts. There was always a faint reek of alcohol and a constant loud hum, like the roar of a distant ocean, from the enormous generator that provided the electrical power for the school.

This was America in 1950. We were the invisible ones, the immigrant refugees, never noticed by the wealthy boys and parents of this exclusive private school, nor remarked upon by the faculty who ministered to their needs. We moved about silently in the shadows. We didn't show ourselves unless required. We were summoned by our first names, which our benefactors assumed was a sign of friendship, but due to the formality of our own social customs, served to remind us of our lowly status. Like our ancestors in nineteenth-century Estonia, once more we were servants to the lords, and relished our freedom during their absence.

Ema was intent on observing an Estonian Christmas in this foreign land. After considerable searching, she managed to procure the proper ingredients for *sült* and *verivorst* from the village butcher. I fondly recalled these Christmas Eve treats from my former life—the small round mounds of cold jelled pork, the crisply fried sausages. This year, however, I made an unfortunate and disgusting discovery. Opening the refrigerator door, I found the source of both: the severed head of a pig was staring out at me with its little squinty eyes.

After boiling the head for many hours, Ema and Nelli picked off the meat, covered it with liquid stock and poured the mixture into a multitude of small bowls which they then set out on the back steps to cool until the hardened fat could be skimmed off. They had forgotten Fritz, with his long nose and fine sense of smell. By the time the little dog was discovered, he had consumed five and a half bowls of *sült*, fat and all.

"OI, OI, OI!" wailed Nelli. "Jeesus Kristus! We have poisoned the fine little gentleman."

Ema was worried too, but after a day and a night of flowing freely from both ends, Fritz survived.

There was also baking to be done. I helped with the *kringle*—a braided loaf loaded with nuts and raisins—and cut rounds from rolled out gingerbread dough for *pipparkook*. Eerik, being the youngest male and judged the hardiest, hauled in a huge fir tree that he cut from the forest surrounding the school. Ema brought out the ornaments she had purchased from the basement of G. Fox and Company the last time we took the bus to Hartford on her day off. She had inquired after candleholders also, but was informed by a snippy girl with frizzy hair and bright lipstick that America had regulations and people used electric lights on their Christmas trees. Nevertheless, we needed to have them, for it had become our solemn duty to keep alive traditions no longer allowed in Communist Estonia. Ema bought two boxes of household candles and Peeter fashioned holders from wire clothes hangers.

Gathered in the headmaster's parlour at an exclusive private school in Connecticut, dressed in our best, we celebrated our first Christmas Eve in the new land. I don't recall our own outfits, mine or my mother's, or Nelli's, but I remember the men's shabby ill-fitting *Laager* suits, which they wore whenever they weren't working—Joosep in his tight-fitting black shiny serge; Peeter in baggy beige gabardine, and Eerik in dark brown moth-eaten tweed.

In Estonia, the holidays had been celebrated for three full days, starting with a church service. We made do with Ema's reading of the Christmas story from Nelli's Estonian Bible and a verse about Baby Jesus recited by me. After murmuring the Lord's Prayer together, we stood up to sing the Estonian National Anthem, all three verses—something Estonian refugees did on every possible occasion. There was a long moment of stunned silence when we finished as if we had lost our bearings, until my mother clapped her hands and herded us into the dining room. We took our places on the high-backed chairs around the long table set with the Prouts' finest silver and china, to feast on roast pork with browned potatoes and carrots, beet salad, pickled herring with sour cream, *sült* and blood sausage (both of which I refused to eat—*You really are a Tita!* my mother scolded), followed by *kringel* and *pipparkook*. Joosep uncorked a bottle of vodka, a special treat only for grown-ups, refilling the small crystal glasses whenever someone shouted out *Proosit*. Each time they emptied a glass, the men smacked their lips and said *Ecch* while Ema and Nelli would make ugly faces and quickly reach for a piece of pickled herring to take away the taste. It made me wonder why anyone would drink something that tasted so horrible.

After dinner, we returned to the parlour where Ema lit all the candles on the tree. According to custom, we each picked one. The person whose candle outlasted the rest would have the longest life. We broke off small branches to singe in the flames, and because the tree was freshly cut, the twigs would merely smoulder, releasing a familiar sweet-smelling incense. Peeter started humming an old Estonian carol, and we all joined in. For an hour or more we sang together, the candlelight reflecting from our unshed tears.

In Estonia, *Jõuluvana* delivered the presents on Christmas Eve. Small children were expected to memorize a verse to recite before receiving their gifts, but often he had arrived when everyone was still in church and the gifts were under the tree upon their return. When I was very little, however, and we still lived in our home on

Rosencrantz Avenue, I performed to *Jõuluvana* in person. Twice. Both times my father happened to be in the bathroom when there was a knock on our door. Outside stood a tall, red-suited stranger with a white beard carrying a large burlap sack. I was terrified, but managed to perform well enough to receive a pat on the head and many presents. Sometime later I found the red suit and whiskers hidden in a trunk in the spare room where Memme slept. It was then I began to suspect that I was not being told the truth about what was really happening in the world.

As I was almost eleven now, this whole charade was omitted. Nevertheless, Christmas is for children, Ema said, and as I was now the only child in the castle, there were many gifts around the tree for me. A pretty handkerchief surrounded with lace and a box of chocolates from Joosep. An Estonian hat knit by Nelli. A colouring book and a box of sixty-four crayons from Peeter and Eerik. Two books written in English, both about dogs—Lad and Lassie—from the Prouts, and a necklace of coloured beads from Baby Lil.

But that wasn't all.

Ema ordered me to close my eyes. I heard her leave the room and then come back.

"You can look now, Totsu," she said,

She had wheeled in a bicycle. Brand new. Bright red. For me. She must have saved for a very long time to buy it.

As the candles burned out one by one that Christmas Eve, my mother's stayed lit the longest. She won the contest and I was glad. I wanted her to live forever. She was the only one I had and she had only me.

It can now be said with a degree of certainty that she truly has proven herself to be the winner in that particular race. Of that ragged company spending our first Christmas together in the new land, only Ema and I remain. The rest were extinguished long ago.

26.
Pop Culture

I LOVED BABY LIL. Everyone did. She had a closet full of beautiful party dresses, bookshelves crammed with books, and so many toys she could never play with them all. She was destined for the best education in expensive private schools, debutante balls, a degree in the Arts from Vassar, a wealthy husband, three brilliant sons, and a beautiful home in Westchester County not far from where I had long ago visited the Maxwells. As grown-ups, we no longer kept in touch except for Christmas cards. Despite all these advantages, her life turned tragic. She suffered from debilitating back pain and became addicted to prescription drugs. The final communication between us took place a few months before she died from an overdose.

I still have a book you made for me when you were ten and I was just a baby, she wrote on the bottom of her Christmas card. *Do you realize that I have known you and your mother longer than anyone else who is left in the world?*

The winter when I was almost eleven, Baby Lil not quite two, and Ema still a servant, I began to feel as though I too belonged in the castle—within the shadows, to be sure, unseen, unknown by those who passed through, but no longer a stranger. Like a mouse, rather, scurrying along corridors, hiding inside walls, aware of the territory. My shiny new red bicycle that I named Josephine stood in the narrow hallway between our room and the stairs. Although I wasn't allowed to take her outside until the snow melted, I would sit on the seat and place my feet on the pedals to practise keeping my balance without touching the walls. It was, in a way, like learning to swim.

When the boys left for spring break, Ema and I carried Josephine to the lawn in front of the Headmaster's Residence.

"We'll try it on the grass first, Totsu," she advised. "Don't worry. I'll be right behind you to keep you steady and I won't let go."

But I already knew how. With my feet pumping furiously, I was off, leaving my astonished mother far behind. Though she shouted something, I didn't look back, pretending not to hear. I was on my own. Speeding down the flagstone paths to the gravelled driveway that led to Patty Whynot's house.

Patty's father was the maintenance foreman. She lived with her mother and father in the Chicken Coop, a wooden structure at the edge of the school grounds containing four apartments. Though not in keeping with the architecture of the other buildings, it accommodated the overflow, housing staff and junior faculty in line for more auspicious quarters. The school nurse lived there, and the headmaster's secretary, and, some years later, Ema and I. It was far enough away from the main campus to escape notice. From here we could ride our bikes directly on to the public road and once even to town, which Ema said was too dangerous. Patty's bike was named Myrtle.

The Whynots were from Nova Scotia, Canada, so Patty was an immigrant too, although her family had always spoken English and was not forced to leave their home because of a war. Her father decided to move to the United States so he could make more money and have a better life. He was building a house for them a few miles from campus, but since he was doing it all by himself it was taking a long time. Patty missed Nova Scotia and the small village by the seashore where men went out fishing, women stayed at home, and everyone was related to everyone else in one way or another.

Patty Whynot was in Grade Eight and a devoted fan of pop culture, which was in no way similar to that promoted by Dr. POP, Sir, nor approved of by my mother. Patty taught me things I would otherwise never have known. On Friday nights, she listened to *Hit Parade* on the radio playing the ten most popular songs of the week. She had magazines with the words of all the current hits printed out which we'd take turns singing. If the tunes weren't familiar, we'd make them up. My favourites were "Aba Daba Honeymoon," "Come On a-My House," and "Shrimp Boats is a Comin'." Patty liked "Mockin' Bird Hill." We also cut out pictures of our favourite stars from the movie magazines Patty collected. She had a boyfriend picked out, so I chose one also—MacDonald Carey. Not a wise selection, I soon discovered, for he never became very popular and there weren't many pictures of him. Patty's boyfriend was George Montgomery. He acted in Westerns mostly and wasn't too famous either, though we both remained loyal.

During the construction of their new home, Patty's parents accumulated many catalogues. The ones from Sears and Roebuck were the fattest. We each took a side of the page to choose the one thing we would most like to own. Sometimes we made the game competitive—whoever pointed to an item first anywhere on the page got it. Consumerism with its awesome power was beginning to taint our innocent young lives even then.

Patty was given an allowance every week and spent every cent of it on magazines and comics. She had huge piles of them under her bed. I preferred *Archie*; she liked *True Romances* best. My mother considered all comic books trash and forbade me to read them. I was not allowed to chew gum either. It was a vulgar American habit, she said, and she did not want me to become Americanized. Popular music was also banned. Our radio was tuned to the FM station which only played classical, or what she referred to as *beautiful music*. In the afternoons when Baby Lil was taking a nap and Ema was on her break, she *did* switch the radio to AM and listened to soap operas (*Stella Dallas*; *Mary Noble, Backstage Wife*; *Lorenzo Jones and His Wife, Belle*) but no one except me knew that.

The Whynots had a TV, a relatively new item at the time for poorer folk. I was permitted to go to Patty's one night a week to watch *I Love Lucy*. I wondered why the Prouts didn't have one, for they were certainly rich enough. Ema explained that Mrs. POP considered it a waste of time and would allow a TV into the house *only over her dead body*.

I could tell that my mother didn't really like the Whynots.

She made it quite obvious to me that they were not up to her standards and she suspected Patty might be a bad influence on me, like Amanda Benton. But as we lived too far away from any of my other schoolmates, and I was under strict instructions to keep away from the prep school boys, she could hardly prevent us from spending time together.

In the 1950s, there was a definite class structure in America that had to do with *quality*. Expensive clothing, an upscale home address, the family name, the country club you belonged to, where you prepped, what college you attended—all played a part; but even if a stranger should appear before you totally naked, it would still be apparent in the stance, the manner of speech and the attitude. I had no doubt that the main reason Ema took the job at the prep school was because of the cultural advantages. She wanted me to grow up among educated people, people of refinement and elegance, like those she used to associate with in her former life. Like the Director of the architectural firm where she worked. Like Onu Gusti. Like some of her friends in *Laager*. She considered the majority of Americans lacking in culture. Like the Bentons. Like Mr. Hooey. Like the Whynots, although they were actually from Canada. Despite her initial lowly position as a waitress and then as a servant, Ema was a snob, and there was hardly a place in America which defined snobbery more precisely than the environment of an exclusive preparatory school in the East. I longed to be a snob myself, but lacked the necessary accoutrements—the cashmere sweaters, the single strand of real pearls, the camel hair coat; not to mention the confidence, the outlook, the upper class accent, the ease and casualness provided by good breeding.

In a university sociology course, we were given the following criteria:

Low class: low income, poor housing, little education.

Middle class: professionals, own a house (mortgaged) a new car (monthly payments), some higher education.

Upper class: inherited money, property, investments.

Tentatively I raised my hand.

"How about low income, poor housing, and a lot of education? How about a DP?"

"Lower class."

"You're wrong," I blurted out, surprising myself by my boldness.

Yet it could be that the professor was right. Scrimping, saving, studying, working hard, graduating at the top of the class, earning the Ph.D., the M.D., the L.LB, none of that made you a part of the truly elite. Not in New England. Not then. Perhaps not even now. Your name would give you away, or the colour of your skin, or your parents who never did learn how to speak English properly and refused to give up their ethnic proclivities. Nelli and Joosep worked at the prep school for years in their lowly positions until they saved enough to buy a mink farm together. In the last Christmas card Nelli sent to my mother, she enclosed a smiling snapshot of herself in a full length white mink coat. But she remained Nelli, dressed up as someone else. No matter what they accomplished, they were immigrants. Future generations might feel they belonged, for it is a nation of immigrants after all, but those of us who were once DPs would bear that label always, even if only in our own consciousness.

"It must have been so hard to bring up a child all by yourself in a new country," I remark to Ema in an unguarded moment during one of our yearly visits.

I expect some self-pity, or at least an acknowledgment of the hardships she endured, but her reply surprises me.

"You gave me a purpose in life. If I didn't have you, I may have not been able to go on."

One of our better exchanges. Still, I never should have started it, for any reference to our past inevitably spoiled the present.

"I wanted so much more for you, Totsu," she continues, appraising with her critical eye my impoverished circumstances in an old farmhouse in Canada. "I wanted you to have a normal life."

She is not impressed by the bouquet of wildflowers on the table, nor the fresh produce from my garden, nor the fact that, after my divorce, I am bringing up three children on my own. She has hoped for something better for us and blames me for not fulfilling her expectations.

You should have...

You could have...
Why didn't you...
Why did you...
Why have you never listened to you mother, Tita?

As usual, I cover up my hurt feelings with a cold indifference and do not give her the hug she deserves.

27.
New Fears

IN 1950, ANOTHER WAR BEGAN. This one took place on the other side of the world, in Korea. It lasted for three years, ending in a stalemate not far from where it started with approximately four million casualties.

Although no bombs had been dropped in America, precautions were taken in case of a nuclear attack. In school, there were drills. Whenever the loudspeaker announced an air raid alert, we were required to *quickly and quietly* line up and walk in single file to the basement corridor, where the boys crouched along the wall on one side and the girls on the other. Even while facing the threat of extinction, it was important to protect our virtue. We kept our heads down and our eyes covered; otherwise the blast would blind us. If we ever happened to see a sudden brilliant light due to a surprise attack, leaving no time for an announcement over the school loudspeaker, we were to crawl underneath our desks. We practised this scenario also.

Once the drills became routine, some of the more waggish boys dared to fool around by making farting sounds, which always produced extensive titters. As a protective measure against such unacceptable behaviour, we were herded into the auditorium and forced to watch documentary films about what it was *really* like—that dreaded mushroom cloud—and what it could do to annihilate a civilization, as had been witnessed in Nagasaki and Hiroshima. To protect their more innocent sensibilities, children in the lower grades were shown cartoons depicting body parts flying in all directions into a bright blue sky. We all took the threat much more seriously after that.

Forward-looking adults were preparing for the final holocaust by building shelters stocked with canned goods and containers of water, secured with sturdy locks so no one else could get in when the catastrophe occurred. After the hydrogen bomb was perfected, either side could activate weapons that would destroy the entire world by merely pushing a button. Fortunately, both leaders also had a red telephone and three minutes in which to call it all off. This is what we were told. I prayed that President Eisenhower wouldn't be on the golf course, where he seemed to spend most of his time and added "the end of the world" to my long list of terrors, which by now included werewolves and murderers and that my mother might find a man in America to replace Onu Gusti. What terrified me most, however, was that if anything happened to Ema, I would be left with no one to look after me.

In the sixties, after a glass of wine, I finally begin to voice my opinions out loud. "Why do some need so much, while others have so little? Why can't we share our wealth equally?"

"*Pfui*, Tita, that sounds like communism," Ema replies.

"I don't believe in -isms, I don't believe in amassing weapons of destruction to destroy the world many times over. I don't believe in war."

"You have to believe in something. What *do* you believe in?"

There were some precepts I had been taught when young that I still do believe—*thou shall not kill* being one, but to avoid a prolonged argument I say nothing more and crawl back into my shell while she continues to contemplate me with her piercing blue eyes.

But when I was almost eleven and we only had each other, my mother and I got along famously most of the time. After Baby Lil was put to bed and Ema's daily chores were finished, we would often lay out a game of double solitaire like she and Tädi Leena used to in *Laager*. Once a month, on her day off, we'd catch a ride to town early in the morning and take the bus to Hartford. There we would wander through the basements of large department stores looking for bargains and take in the matinee at

State Theater, a tawdry version of New York's Radio City Music Hall. We would sit through two films—one in Technicolor, the other a black and white B movie—plus a stage show, sometimes featuring a famous performer. We saw Gordon McCrae there. He sat alone on the stage wearing a cowboy hat and sang a few songs accompanying himself on a guitar. When we emerged bleary-eyed from the darkness of the theatre, it was dark outside also. We would then take the bus back and call a taxi from the corner drugstore to drive us the three miles to the prep school.

Often we sang together, Ema and I. Mostly old Estonian songs that she had taught me. Ema was a good singer and would harmonize to my childish soprano. Sometimes we did it just for fun. Like in the mornings, if we weren't in too much of a rush.

TERE HOMMIKUT! one of us would sing out—Good Morning.
Tere hommikut, the other sang in reply.
TERE HOMMIKUT!
Tere hommikut,
TERE, TERE, TERE, TERE! TERE, TERE, TERE, TERE!
TERE, TERE, TERE, TERE, TERE HOMMIKUT!

Ema did the *tere-tere-tere's* so much better than I ever could. Like a bird twittering.

We also sang KRAMBAMBULI, my favourite, the one I had sung with Isa.
KAS ON SEE NII?
Ja, muidugi.
SIIS LAULAME
Krambambuli
(Together, very loudly) KRAM-BIM-BAM-BAMBULI. KRAMBAM-BULI!

We sang in English too, songs from the musical comedies Ema and I both adored.
Anything you can do, I can do better.
i can do anything better than you.
No you can't.
YES I CAN.
No you can't.
YES I CAN. YES I CAN. YES I CA-AN!

Of course, Ema could do everything better. She was my mother.

Sometimes, not too often, I truly felt that I wanted to hug and kiss her, and I did.

In the summer, the Prouts rented a cottage at the seashore for a month. They took us along so Ema could take care of Baby Lil and do the household chores. I was looking forward to this vacation, expecting something like my visit to the Maxwells, but it was not at all the same. The house was on top of a high cliff that gave a good view of the ocean. Because of the fierce undertow however, it was impossible to swim there even if one did manage to clamber down the rocks to the water. The Prouts took Baby Lil to the nearby private beach, where we weren't allowed, so I occupied myself with reading. On her day off, Ema and I went to the public beach further down the road. She lay on a towel to sunbathe while I spent entire afternoons in the water. Shy as I was, it wasn't hard to meet other kids, for we seemed to gravitate together, jumping over the waves.

Fairly proficient in English by this time, I would attempt a new identity.

I'm Betty, I'd say (or Jane, or Judy, or Sara).

Sometimes I'd forget who I was.

Hey Betty! someone would shout. *Are you deaf or something?*

But most of the time it worked, and, immersed up to my neck in the ocean, I felt like any other kid. Until Ema came to call me out of the water, gabbling in Estonian. I'd pretend not to hear, but someone would always point her out to me.

That woman wants you, Jane. Who is she? What's she saying?

I could feel them gaping after me as I waded out of the water to become myself once again. *That girl is really weird*, I heard them thinking. And I was. I was.

Only Estonians could pronounce my real given name correctly. Most everyone else said *What? Say that again? How do you spell it? What kind of a name is that? Where are you from anyway? Estonia? The Stone Age? Hardy-har-har. Never heard of it.*

After we returned from the seashore, Ema had two weeks off and we took the bus to Lakewood, New Jersey to visit Tädi Leena and Annie-Mannie whom we hadn't seen since we left Germany. The fourteen hour bus ride seemed to transport us right back to *Laager*. Hundreds of Estonians lived in the barrack-like enclosures housing the employees of Seabrook Farms. The women packed and processed vegetables; the men laboured in the fields. Although the children of the workers were enrolled in the public school system, Estonians kept their offspring firmly leashed to the native culture through Scout and Guide groups, folk dancing troupes, choirs, church, and even an Estonian school on Saturday mornings. No one was becoming Americanized here.

Onu Karl looked about the same. The older brother had become a grown-up. Tädi Leena was much heavier, perhaps due to an addiction to Corn Flakes, which she consumed by large bowlfuls at every opportunity. Annie-Mannie had changed the most. She was thin and pretty, taller than me, with long brown hair. She didn't have to wear glasses like I did. It was as though we had changed places. She had a lot of friends and had gained confidence, whereas I had lost my identity and had not found another. I didn't know what to say or how to act with the Estonian kids. My mind was burdened with all sorts of nonsense in two languages which both seemed foreign to me.

I no longer belonged anywhere. I hated myself. And I hated my mother also. It was her fault. Somehow. Yet she seemed happy enough, laughing and chattering in Estonian with her old friend Tädi Leena as they laid out cards for double solitaire like they used to, while I cried myself to sleep.

After this trip, Ema decided that we had become far too secluded. What she needed was better transportation so we could participate more in Estonian activities. Above all else, she did not want her daughter to become Americanized. Although she had never in her life driven an automobile, she bought a 1939 light blue Dodge sedan with running boards and plush beige velvet seats for fifty dollars. She named it *Blue Baby* and practised driving around the gravel roads of the school property. There were a few mishaps. One time she locked the keys in the car. Another time she left the emergency brake on and putted along for quite some distance before she noticed a strange smell and saw smoke billowing out of *Blue Baby*'s innards. Right away she stopped and ran to the other side of the road in case of an explosion. But the smoke soon drifted away and both she and the automobile survived.

Outside the confines of the school, our closest Estonian neighbours were the Otts. They had owned a large farm in Estonia and were lucky enough to be sponsored by a wealthy insurance executive who needed someone as a caretaker for his small hobby farm. It was a beautiful place on a hilltop overlooking Hartford, with a barn and a few animals, large gardens, and fields. The master spent most of his time in his town house, so the Otts and their two teenaged sons were able to regard the place almost as their own, as if they had travelled back in time to a feudal society before the onset of the Industrial Revolution and the great upheavals of the twentieth century.

After six months of daily practice, my mother got her driver's license and took her first trip off the school property over the winding back roads to visit the Otts. Her primary motivation was to play bridge, for the Otts were as fanatical about the game as she was. For many years thereafter, they got together every weekend and sometimes during the week as well. In fact, we spent so much time with the Otts during our first decade in America that I looked upon them almost as family. When, to the great distress of my mother and the Estonian community, I didn't stay true to my heritage but married an American, it was Papa Ott who walked me down the aisle to "give me away."

Since Ema now had a car, we were able to visit Estonians in other parts of Connecticut as well—a dentist, a judge, a professor and his wife, and a Lutheran minister who was preparing to start up an Estonian congregation—every one of them working at menial jobs until mandatory retirement age (this being seventy-five for those who had subtracted ten years from their age to improve their chances of immigration). The judge, Härra Pilves, spent his nights in a bakery and his afternoons doing political research. I liked visiting there because he always brought home fresh donuts and paid attention to me, treating me as a grown-up. Hr. Pilves belonged to the John Birch Society and was very fond of a man named Senator Joseph McCarthy, who, he said, was the only politician smart enough to fight Communism in America, the rest being either *dupes* or *slightly pink*. There were

Communist infiltrators everywhere, he said—in public schools, in universities, in the media and entertainment industries, all trying to influence the hearts and minds of the ignorant and naïve. He gave examples from many films, even from some of the musicals that Ema and I liked so much, claiming that they were full of Communist propaganda. If we weren't watchful, the Communists would take over the country from the inside without having to drop a single bomb.

Hr. Pilves conspired to enlist me as a spy. All I would have to do was to write down anything my teacher said that was critical of the United States of America. He gave me a list of questions I should ask *to help a little immigrant girl understand about the new country.* From the answers, it would be easy to tell if the teacher was *a Communist sympathizer.*

For a while I tried spying, but there didn't seem to be anything much to report. Hr. Pilves suggested that Ema come to my class to give a speech to set everyone straight about what Communism is really like. Surprisingly she agreed, but the teacher didn't want anything to do with it, *not with Senator McCarthy on the loose.*

There was a lot of talk on the radio about Senator McCarthy.

"I do not like his means, but I like his ends," was Ema's opinion.

Some real spies, the Rosenbergs, were going to be executed. Their two sons, both younger than me, made a public plea for their parents' lives. Hr. Pilves called it propaganda, saying that sort of thing would never be broadcast if the Communists didn't control the media.

I came to understand that there are far more dangers in the world than one could ever imagine. It was foolish to believe that there was a God who would protect me from all of them. Yet I was too frightened to stop praying altogether.

28.
Cinderella

FOR THE REMAINDER of my time in elementary school, I spent the day reading Nancy Drew mysteries under my desk in the classroom and finished them under my bedclothes with the help of a flashlight at night. Nancy, George, and Beth became the friends I didn't have, for even Patty Whynot had moved away to the new house her father built. In sturdy Oxfords and serviceable hand-me-downs from Mrs. POP that Ema altered to fit me, I walked a half mile to the bus stop, yearning for the penny-loafers, short-sleeved Orlon sweaters and full cotton skirts that the other girls wore.

We had been in the United States a little over two years when my mother's guardian angel appeared to her once again. Not in the form of Mr. Hooey this time, but as Proua Kiis, the wife of the Estonian minister. She telephoned my mother, which was unusual in itself, as we didn't receive many phone calls. There was a job advertisement in *The Hartford Times*, she said. The prep school where we lived needed a bookkeeper.

"Why don't you apply?" Pr. Kiis urged.

"Oh no, I couldn't," Ema said, succumbing to the immigrant mentality which considers oneself suitable only for the lowliest occupations.

"Why not? It's your former profession, after all," this new guardian angel insisted.

When you are a DP and an immigrant, it is very easy to forget that you are still the person you once were except in a different language. Luckily, Ema's personality had always been forceful and had been fortified rather than diminished during our four years in *Laager*. Despite her circumstances, she remained true to her nature and was never completely subjugated to servitude. *Get in line, Totsu,* she would urge. *Push ahead. Elbow your way to the front if you must, but politely. Learn. Study. Ask someone who knows to help you. It's always best to be at the top of the heap.* These precepts enabled her to survive in the past, and she continued to employ them to improve our future.

She spent the night in restless sleep, thinking it over. By morning, she had made her decision. Why not indeed?

Nervous but determined, she made an appointment with the headmaster's secretary to meet with him in his private office.

"Mrs. Prout will not be happy about this," Dr. POP said slowly, leaning back into the soft cushions of his leather chair and tapping out the ashes from his pipe.

Ema kept her eyes down out of respect. She suspected correctly that he was more in need of a bookkeeper than a housemaid. There were plenty of other DPs available to take over her old position.

"But we shall try you out," he offered, standing up and shaking her hand. "Why not?"

I heard her revealing all this on the telephone to Pr. Kiis that evening.

The next day Ema went to work at the Business Office, armed with her enormously fat *Silvet's English-Estonian Dictionary* published in Sweden in 1946, which she bought in Augsburg and which had traveled with us from Germany (along with the manual about chicken farming). There she soon impressed everyone with her acumen and skill. As I myself had found out in the Foster Center School, mathematics overcomes all linguistic differences.

Henceforth she was called "Ma'am," just like Mrs. Prout, and was addressed respectfully by her surname. We moved from the headmaster's castle to a one-bedroom apartment in the Chicken Coop, where I formerly visited Patty Whynot. As we no longer lived on the main campus where the boys might be distracted by my legs or my underwear, I was now allowed to wear shorts and hang my wash on the clothesline. Furniture was provided, but it was ornate and Victorian, in keeping with the architecture of the school, and not to Ema's taste. She preferred *simple elegance* and had always harboured a secret longing to be an interior decorator. With her meagre savings, she bought two modern Danish chairs and a matching sofa that unfolded into a bed. For the first time since we left our home on Rosencrantz Avenue, my mother and I slept in separate rooms.

She also bought a sewing machine, and we discovered Myrtle Mills, a discount store offering wonderful deals on remnants. It was thrilling to unfold a new piece of fabric, spread it out on the floor, pin on the tissue paper pattern, and cut out shapes from crisp polished cotton with pinking shears. I already knew how to baste and hem and sew on buttons, skills I had learned in *Laager*. Ema showed me how to sew straight seams on the new machine, how to make darts and gathers, and, most difficult of all, how to fit in zippers so they hardly showed. We didn't bother with buttonholes. We always chose the patterns labelled *Easy-to-Make*.

To celebrate my twelfth birthday, Ema took me to see Walt Disney's *Cinderella,* after which I began desperately to wish for a Fairy Godmother of my own. My transformation was painfully slow however, with no magic wand or *Bibbidi-Babbadi-Boo* to bring it to fruition. Eventually the round black-framed metal glasses I wore were replaced by a new pink plastic pair, the closet gradually filled with homemade skirts and dresses, buds of breasts became embarrassingly noticeable under my T-shirts and sweaters, and hair began sprouting where none had been before. Longing for my Prince to come, I was Tita all the time now.

Ema's salary included room and also board when school was in session, so we ate most of our meals at the Refectory with the rest of the school community. My deadly sin of vanity was well-nourished and fertilized during the nightly muss and fluster as I prepared myself for my grand entrance into the dining room at six o'clock each evening. After constant nagging, Ema had finally conceded about my glasses and agreed I didn't need to wear them for eating. In my new polished cotton circle skirt, white bobby socks and penny-loafers, the only girl among more than two hundred adolescent boys, I sat self-consciously beside my mother in my assigned place at the long oaken table. Because I thought it disfiguring to chew, it didn't take me long to lose my baby fat.

Even though our apartment was very small, consisting of a bedroom, a tiny kitchen, and the living room where my mother slept on the fold-out couch, she managed to fit in an old upright piano that she bought for twenty dollars, and I began lessons once again. Fidgety old Mrs. Spark came every Tuesday afternoon for a half an hour to listen to what I had practised the previous week and to assign a new piece. However, due to Patty Whynot's influence, and much to my mother's dismay, I greatly preferred popular music and spent the small portion of my babysitting money not saved for college on sheet music—"Tell Me Why" (The Four Aces), "Lady of Spain" (Eddie Fisher), "Tennessee Waltz" (Patti Page, the Singing Rage) and my favourite, "Give Me a Kiss to Build a Dream On." I sang along to that one, dedicating it to dark-eyed Rinaldo, called "Chico," a foreign student from Cuba who sometimes sat at our table. *Hey amigo, pass the rolls to that buutiful blonde,* I once heard him say, and, although he never spoke to me directly, he stole my heart like Ints had in *Laager* long ago.

In the 1950s, life was divided into very clearly defined periods. You were a baby, a toddler, a child. Then you were a kid going through eight years of elementary school until you become a teenager. When you left high school, you became all grown-up, unless you elected higher education, in which case you were "a college kid." People in their thirties were "over the hill," and those beyond fifty were "old folks." Everyone was expected to act in accordance to his age. *Act your age, Tita.*

Although Ema promoted freedom as the most important aspect of life—for her country and herself—she regarded me as a colony under her sole control and domination. Except when I attended school, we were always together so she could keep an eye on me. And this she did. If I had any thoughts or feelings of my own, they seemed disloyal. Totsu was a good girl. Tita had become not only a nuisance, but subversive as well. The evil twin.

By the early fifties, there were close to five hundred Estonians living in various parts of Connecticut. A National Expatriate Committee was formed. The Estonian minister began to conduct services in Lutheran churches all around the state. A choir was started, and Ema drove an hour's distance once a week to attend rehearsals, dragging me along. In the factory town of Willimantic, where many immigrants had found jobs, the Polish Hall was occasionally rented to celebrate special occasions such as the Estonian Independence Day. The program would consist of patriotic speeches, declamations, and musical performances, followed by a dance with music provided by an Estonian accordionist. Not old enough to join the Otts' two sons at the "young people's table," I would sit miserably beside my mother at these events, a wallflower, watching others having fun and hoping that maybe someone, a boy or even an old man, would notice me and ask me for a dance.

The week before my elementary school graduation, our class was given a booklet entitled *Hi There, High School!* It specified what we should wear, how we should behave, what activities we could join, what sports would be offered, what would be expected of us and how much fun it would all be. During that summer, when I was thirteen, I read it through many times and could hardly wait. Finally I would have the opportunity to truly reinvent myself.

After a great deal of persistent haggling about what I should be permitted now that I was a teenager, Ema began to relent. She gave us both a home permanent—a Toni. It turned out frizzy, but I thought it definitely made me look older. She also let me put on a bit of her lipstick for special occasions. I got my first girdle and stockings, and, most significantly, a bra. Secretly I began to shave my legs and armpits, for Ema never would have consented to that. I only wore my glasses at home and only if she reminded me. *Where are your glasses, Tita?*

Fairy godmother or not, I was ready.

29.
The Cold War

AN IMMIGRANT CHILD is always split between the new and the old. At home, you speak a different language, use different manners, sing different songs; the intonations of your speech, the way you dance, your mode of dress, how you interact with others, the food you eat, the opinions you are expected to hold, even your sense of humour, all are determined and controlled by a different culture. Your speech, learned in infancy, is dependent on the way you position your tongue and teeth and the tension of your lips. Estonians are a subdued people, never opening their mouths very wide, lips clamped to the teeth instead of pursed outward (as compared to Americans, or, even more so to the French). Viewing those old-fashioned home movies where the loud whir of the projector provides the only sound, I could always tell if Ema and I were speaking Estonian or English simply by observing how our mouths moved. Early on I made the discovery that in order to truly acclimate to a new culture, you have to embrace it not only with your mind but with your entire body, or you'll spend your whole life in a state of translation.

During my adolescence, I viewed my mother as a continual intrusion in my pursuit of happiness, cringing with embarrassment whenever she called out my name or spoke Estonian to me in public. I wanted to shake her off, to shoo her away. I wanted to be American like everyone else. In the consolidated high school I attended, most students were unaware of my ignominious arrival and hadn't witnessed my struggles and humiliations as a DP. I looked like any other thirteen-year-old girl in my ankle-length skirt (though I made mine myself), topped by a short-sleeved sweater with a small scarf tied in a square knot around my neck (often pinned with a display of artificial flowers), wearing white cotton socks and penny loafers. Only my name gave me away.

We were *High School Kids*.

Upon entrance, we were divided into three groups—*Collegiate, Secretarial, Industrial*—which determined not only our friends and our preoccupations, but the entire course of our subsequent lives. We carried our books carelessly in front of our emerging breasts instead of in book bags. We wore our socks rolled down and our dungarees rolled up. "Blackboard Jungle" didn't reach the movie screens until 1955, when "Rock Around the Clock" changed popular music forever. We still cried along with Johnnie Ray as he sobbed out his first big hit "Cry" and swooned over Eddie Fisher. Though we succumbed to parental authority, our teenage angst was evidenced by frequent sulking and an obviously snotty attitude.

You really are a Tita, Ema often said in exasperation, sounding surprised, as if there hadn't been numerous signposts along the way that she had never neglected to point out to me. Obedient I was still, but, oh boy, did I resent it! She sounded so stupid. I hated her accent, the way she said *Jaa*, and *Dank you very much* and *I beg your pardon*. She was a lot smarter in Estonian, but Americans didn't know that.

In high school, I was lucky enough to find a best friend—someone to depend upon, to giggle with, to confide in, and to cling to as we withstood the formidable and unknown world that lay ahead of us. Having retained my desire for stardom, I immediately joined the Drama Club and was chosen for the leading role in the annual school production over Annabel Mayor, a Senior noted for her dramatic flair, who also read for the part. This time I didn't play a DP, although our experience of servitude may have given me the edge I needed. I was Dora, the Beautiful Dishwasher, and a resounding hit. Everyone in school knew me after that. The most popular boy in our class asked me to the Winter Dance. It was our first and only date, but from that time on my social standing was assured.

Yet I lived in three different worlds and felt like a stranger in each one.

The exclusive community of the prep school promoted the upper-class traditions of nineteenth-century England. Except on weekends, students were expected to wear suits and ties (grey for class, blue for dinner and formal occasions), the faculty affected a slight British accent, and Sir and Ma'am were the common forms of address. Due to the elevation of my mother's status, we were now able to take advantage of all the cultural accoutrements the campus provided. In addition to the candlelit three-course dinner every night, there were evenings of chamber music in the Prouts' elegant parlour, frequent theatrical performances and concerts in the Refectory, plus art exhibits, lectures, and elaborate festivals celebrating holidays in the Victorian manner. Winter and Spring Dance Weekends were the social highlights of the school year. Dates arrived from all parts of the United States and also from the nearby private girls' schools. I was always invited by someone, but felt like a bargain basement substitute among all these rich girls, not a debutante in cashmere and pearls, not a guest of the school, but picked up at the Chicken Coop, my ball gown a hand-me-down. Finally a Cinderella, but too conscientious to lose a shoe and feeling more comfortable among the cinders.

Many years later, that familiar New England upper class twang could still bring back my insecurities (*Who is that? Nobody*), a momentary lapse before I regained my adult identity. Even Ema, during the remainder of her long life, always employed a different tone of voice when referring to "rich people." Although she might deny it, I am certain that she never truly overcame the subjugation we endured as DPs either.

Well, they're wealthy, you know, Tita, she'd remark, which, given my proclivities, I viewed as a criticism of my failure to achieve that coveted status, despite all the opportunities she had provided for me.

Although my mother made many American friends over the years, she spent most of her leisure time with Estonians. We drove great distances to take part in Estonian activities. At Ema's urging, I reluctantly joined the folk dancing troupe and the church choir, but had little in common with other young people who remained much more nationalistic. Most of them eventually ended up married to other Estonians, leaving it to their children to become fully assimilated. The socials were fun, however, for in my teenage years I never lacked for dancing partners as I perfected the polka, the Viennese waltz, the tango, the fox-trot, and the rumba to the familiar strains of the accordion. Still, I would have much rather been with my own high school crowd. Yet even there I didn't really belong, for we weren't part of the local community and I hardly ever saw my friends except at school, and not at all during summer vacations.

Thus each aspect of my adolescence became a part-time role. Switching from one reality to another, there was no time to collect myself, to mature, to consider who I was or wanted to be. I was voted "Most Likely to Succeed," but whatever I did achieve inevitably pointed to my failures. I graduated third in my class, not first; I was a Princess at the Senior Prom, not the Queen; I was accepted at Vassar College but not given a scholarship, so I couldn't afford to go and attended the State University instead. *Anything you can do I can do better, I can do anything better than you*—the theme song of a competitive society. *Only the best is good enough, Totsu. If at first you don't succeed, try, try again. If you didn't win this time, you will the next.* I didn't find out until much later that true satisfaction comes from within.

Although nuclear annihilation was an ever-present danger during these Cold War years, now that I had become a teenager there was another more immediate threat that my mother had warned me about ever since I could remember.

SEX.

The word was hardly ever mentioned within her hearing, but at the slightest whiff of it Ema's mouth would curl into a pinched moue of disgust. This was the 1950s. Navels were airbrushed from underwear ads. Married couples were portrayed as sleeping in twin beds. Torrid love scenes in films consisted of the romantic male lead lighting two cigarettes and placing one between a woman's lips before the fade out.

When she first took the job at the prep school, it is doubtful that Ema had taken full account of the fact that in a very few years I would be the only teenaged girl living among two hundred and fifty adolescent boys. I remained a child in her eyes and she took every possible precaution to protect me from the predatory ways of men, her eagle eyes alert, her claws ready. Whenever possible, she monitored my every action and thought, flipping through the pages of the books I was reading and scrutinizing any notes or correspondence she found to make sure there was no hint of the dreaded subject. I was allowed to go to chaperoned dances, but she would be posted at the window watching for my prompt return.

After raising two daughters and a son myself, I must admit that the watchfulness that seemed so extreme then doesn't seem so extraordinary now. But Ema didn't have to worry, for I had learned my lessons well. *Sex, Pfui.* Unlike most of my girlfriends, I never wore a boy's fat silver ID bracelet around my wrist, his high school ring on a chain around my neck, or his immense white cardigan with an athletic letter sewn on the back, to indicate I was "going steady." I might flirt a bit and suffer through a few unrequited crushes, but if anyone tried to touch me, I immediately withdrew. *May I kiss you goodnight?* NO.

Without Ema's knowledge, her early lessons in propriety were being constantly reinforced in ways she never even suspected by men old enough to be my father or grandfather. The playful pinch, the suggestive joke, the pat on the rear, all in good fun. It soon became obvious which ones to be wary of by a softening in their eyes, a thickening of the voice, a swollen look to the lips. Often, also, the smell of liquor. And the drift of the conversation:

You're what, fourteen now? Getting to be quite a nice-looking young lady. Yessiree. Got a boyfriend?

Uncles, grandpas, fathers of girlfriends. Hugs, gropes, and subverted kisses. Driven home from babysitting, getting a firm grip on the door handle while Daddy fumbled in his trousers for change, his other hand straying over the front seat, searching for my thigh. At first, I thought it must be my fault. Being fatherless, I may have subconsciously craved male attention. Being an immigrant, I was too trusting. From a very young age I had the propensity to flirt. Or perhaps my perverted imagination was making the whole thing up. Yet it was flattering too that these adult males found me so attractive.

Not until women began to talk more freely to each other, did we discover that these secret encounters were by no means unique. At the high school reunion, we shared stories of fingers that inched from shoulder to breast, strayed from waist to buttock, or started a slow creep up from the knee, fingers attached to the hands of teachers, of respectable townsmen, husbands, fathers, neighbours, friends, or occasionally strangers lurking in the dark depths of movie theatres. Every one of us had something to relate. We recollected the slobbery lips of Tina Sawyer's old Gramps, the hard lap of the driver training teacher as he soundly spanked the girls who forgot to signal, the pinch of Mr. Tandy, the math teacher, for wrong answers, or the leering stare of the music teacher, Mr. Withers, zooming in between navel and neck. We had all been treated to the suggestive taunt, the unwanted squeeze, the occasional full-frontal exposure. We didn't complain and we never told. Not in those days. It was only the poor old recluse, Tommy Oickle, caught stealing ladies' underwear from clotheslines, who ever endured a measure of public scorn.

"Remember Härra Pirn, the one who had his hands blown off in the war? He was always groping at me," I reveal to Ema during one my visits.

"You too? Whenever he'd start in on me, I'd shout loudly to his wife: 'Minnie, where do you keep your napkins?' That stopped him. If he had a drink or two, that man was all hands," she remarks wryly.

Ema is ninety-two, I am sixty-four, and we laugh heartily together.

But it was no laughing matter in 1952. When I started my period, Ema asked if there was anything I wanted to know now that *those days* had begun.

"It's okay," I said to ease our mutual embarrassment. "Proua Nelli already told me everything in *Laager*."

And that was the total extent of my sexual education until my first year in university. I was aware that men had something hard in their pants, purple and ugly, but when the opportunity arose some years later to take a look, I actually shielded my eyes from the sight.

Most of the girls in my dorm had steady boyfriends. Others were "wild," even in the hazardous days before the Pill. A sex quiz was being passed around. I scored three points for *kissing a member of the opposite sex on the mouth with the mouth closed.* I could have had three more for *French kissing,* but didn't realize that I had indeed experienced this particular delight at eleven or twelve years of age, when fat old Mr. C., full of Christmas cheer, grabbed a hold of me under the mistletoe. Before I could prepare myself like Ema had showed me—*Purse your lips Tita and make sure your teeth are clamped together*—he stuck the big gristle of his disgusting tongue deeply into my shocked mouth. I almost threw up.

Prior to this quiz, I was beginning to think I was the same as anyone else, a typical co-ed. But obviously I had only assimilated surface behaviour and knew nothing about what people were like off stage, where real life took place, underneath the sheets, so to speak. Many girls had scores of two hundred or more and were proud of it. Possibly some of them were exaggerating to show off, but that didn't prevent me from once again feeling like a *Dumkoff Auslander*. On my own now among all these other people so different from myself, without my mother's constant and domineering interference to protect me, I became painfully shy once again. I kept my distance from the men I found most attractive, those who might possibly endanger my virginity, realizing that the greatest struggle was yet to come—to preserve it at all costs until marriage.

30.
Taat

I SAW MY FATHER one more time before he died. After we left Augsburg, he remained in Germany for a few more years, writing me an occasional letter with photos of himself enclosed and sending an Estonian book for Christmas and my birthdays. These always included a carefully composed inscription on the flyleaf, written in his beautiful penmanship, reminding me never to forget him or our lost homeland that he had spent his youth fighting to protect. Surely I must have replied to thank him, though I don't remember much about our correspondence. In fact, I hardly ever thought of him at all.

Rarely did I allow myself to imagine how wonderful it would be to have a real father, one who took you places, taught you things, and looked upon you lovingly in spite of your imperfections. This had nothing to do with Isa. It was a vague, amorphous longing arising at unexpected moments, an ache somewhere deep within, sentimental and selfish, a hankering for a relationship that rarely existed even for many of my girlfriends who did have fathers. I certainly didn't want Isa to suddenly reappear and move in with us, nor did I want Ema to find someone to replace him or Onu Gusti. Not then. Not while I was still living there. She could do whatever she wanted as soon as I moved away.

By the time DP camps were shut down, Isa too had immigrated to the United States, to a suburb of Chicago. He must have written to tell me this, but our letters had become infrequent and I hardly remember reading them. Although Ema insisted that we always speak our native language with each other so that I would never forget it, reading and writing without any practice became increasingly difficult. The Estonian books Isa sent remained unopened on Ema's bookshelves. I had neither the patience nor the inclination to concentrate on yet another sombre tome about the everlasting suffering of the homeland. I was bored with all the nationalistic brouhaha—the endless ceremonies and speeches, the teary-eyed singing of the national anthem, the constant exhortations directed at the younger generation to remember that it was our sacred duty to preserve the Estonian heritage. In fact, I was prepared to deny the first ten years of my life altogether, to pretend that Ema and Isa and the whole downtrodden Estonian nation never existed, ready and willing to pass myself off as someone born again into a different time and place. I was, in fact, becoming thoroughly Americanized.

Yet it affected me more than I ever thought possible when, at an Estonian gathering, a student from the University of Chicago mentioned to me that he knew my father and had also met his wife and two children. That he had been to their home, in fact, for dinner.

"You must be confusing him with someone else," I replied. "My father and mother are still married, as far as I know. And he only has one child—me!"

I was incensed and told Ema right away, but she took it all very calmly. She wasn't aware he was married again and had children, she said, but neither was she surprised. Volli had always been a ladies' man. She had obtained a divorce before we came to America, so our documents would be in order. It was just a formality, really, as they had lived apart for years. A child must have been on the way even before we left Germany, she speculated, figuring out the numbers in her head. From the tone of her voice and the sour expression on her face, I could tell what she was thinking, although she didn't come right out and say it: *Men are only after one thing, remember that, Totsu.*

"But why didn't he tell me?" I complained. "Why would he keep something like that a secret? He always said I was his dear, beautiful daughter that he missed so much, and now I find out he has a whole other family."

"He always was one for keeping things to himself."

"It's like lying," I complained, "not to tell a person the truth."

"Volli never was good with the truth," she replied curtly, thus ending the conversation.

Her heart had hardened more than mine. She had shut him out of hers a long time before I did, for reasons she had never discussed with me.

I finally wrote him, asking if it was true what I had heard, and, if so, why he had kept it a secret. And he wrote back saying he was nervous about telling me because he knew how jealous I could be. And I wrote saying, no, I had no reason to be jealous, I was just upset that he hadn't told me. He then sent photos of his two children, a girl and a boy, saying that he always talked to them about their beautiful and kind older sister who lived far away and whom they would meet someday. He never mentioned their mother, nor did he ever send a picture of her. I was sure she couldn't have been the actress from Geislingen he brought with him when he came to say goodbye to me at Hochfeld *Laager*. Ema may have been right all along—my father was definitely a ladies' man, not to be trusted.

A more permanent alienation between us took place four years later when I was in my last year in college and sent Isa a clipping from the newspaper announcing my engagement. His response totally shocked me. In his beautiful and controlled script, which had previously only described refined and loving sentiments, he now released the frustrations and disappointments of his life in exile. He was a true patriot. He had been willing to give up his life for his country and refused to become a citizen of any other. I was a soldier's daughter. How could I turn my back on my suffering homeland and my own people in this way? How could I betray my Estonian heritage by marrying an American?

I was insulted and infuriated. How dare he make a judgement upon someone he hadn't laid eyes on in more than ten years and hadn't seen very often before that? I was his daughter, true, but one he had never really known or supported. If he felt so inclined, he could exert his authority upon his other family, and I pitied them. For once, Ema agreed with me, although she was also distressed about my forthcoming marriage.

I never did reply to Isa's outburst. Nevertheless, after a short while he sent me an apology, which must have been very difficult for him but meant nothing to me. I didn't answer that letter either, and we never corresponded again.

Another decade went by.

My husband and I were both university instructors in the Midwest and had two young children when Isa's daughter telephoned. Like Preili Sütt, she had searched out my mother's address by contacting the Estonian Consulate in New York City, and had written to Ema inquiring my whereabouts.

"He's getting old," she said. "He has talked about you ever since I was born. He wants to see you again before he dies. May we come for a visit? I would also love to meet the sister I have never known."

There was no possible way to deny a request like that.

"If he's your Daddy, how come he isn't our Grampa then?" my oldest wanted to know.

I pretended not hear the question. After a quick glance in the mirror to make sure my hair was in place, I went to the kitchen to check on the roast and looked out the window once again.

"Relax," my husband said. "They're probably as nervous as you are."

"I have no reason to be nervous," I snapped at him. "These people are strangers to me. I'm just doing this because I don't know how to get out of it."

When a car pulled in the driveway, I peered out between the slats of the Venetian blind in the hallway, watching his other daughter, a tall slim girl with dark curly hair, dressed casually in tight jeans and stylish boots, emerge from the driver's side. My father wore a tweed sports coat, a knitted vest, and a tie. In my memory, he had always been in uniform. He was also much shorter than I remembered, or perhaps he had shrunk. His hair was grey. He straightened himself as they walked towards the front door. She smiled at him, and I noticed her squeeze his arm in encouragement.

My half-sister was ten years younger than me. In her face, I glimpsed Isa as he used to look, except for her large brown eyes. His were blue. She was stunningly beautiful. I smoothed my hair once again and tugged at my skirt, feeling like a *housefrau*, plain and dumpy. It was too late to hide. Taking a deep breath, I stepped forward to greet them.

"Tere!" the girl cried out in Estonian. "I am your sister." She rushed to hug me.

"Tere, Isa," I said to my father, and we embraced too, hesitantly, like the strangers we were.

"I'm sorry we're late," said the girl. "Taat was so nervous, he kept dawdling." She smiled at him, teasingly. The affection between them was palpable.

Once inside, we switched into English as I introduced my family. The children smiled shyly at this old man, their grandfather, *Taat*. He gave a broad wink to each one before extending his hand to my husband. It soon became apparent that he had lost none of his charm.

We chit-chatted about the externals of our lives, in an attempt to forge some sort of communion. In spite of my fretfulness, dinner turned out well. The meat was tender, vegetables not overcooked, mashed potatoes lumpless, rolls browned and soft, the salad triumphant. Wine flowed freely. Isa brought a bottle of the best. The children were well-behaved, my husband sounded intelligent but not pushy, my half-sister was sensitively supportive as my father and I exchanged furtive glances and attempted tentative verbal encounters.

"Krambambuli!" I cried out impulsively, raising my glass.

"Krambambuli!" the little ones shouted, lifting up their cups of apple juice.

"Krambambuli!" my husband, my father, and my half-sister responded.

Am I the only one who apprehended the significance of this word, recalling Isa, strong and tall, throwing me up into the air to catch me in his arms, only to throw me up once again? *Krambambuli!*

Our eyes met, but I could not tell if he also remembered, or simply considered this some sort of quirky salutation to celebrate the occasion.

They left shortly after, with promises on both sides to meet again soon, the hugs longer and more substantial, the rusty emotions lubricated by wine.

It is only then that our real parting returned to me. Not the final time we last saw each other, when Ema and I left Augsburg, but the day I was forced to remove him from my heart.

Isa. Isa. Isa.

How I loved him then.

His reappearance brought back to me the wonderful, tall, handsome soldier who was my father, who wrote a book for me, who drove such a long way to visit us in *Laager*, who gave me his dog and let me steer his car sitting on his lap on the *Autobahn*. I was crying for him that first time because he could never see me again. Now I wept for what I myself had lost. For all that we might have shared over the years. For everything that could have been and was impossible ever to recapture. Of course he had his flaws. But they had nothing to do with me.

Another war was going on, in Vietnam this time, the longest military conflict in United States history. Twelve to thirteen percent of the total Vietnam population was killed—between three and four million people. To put this figure into a different perspective—thirteen percent of the United States population would equal twenty-eight million dead Americans. In actual fact, fifty-eight thousand one hundred and sixty-nine Americans were killed in action. Their average age was twenty-one. One and a half to two million Cambodians also lost their lives. After ten years of fighting, the American troops withdrew and North and South Vietnam reunited.

The polarization of American society and our personal feelings against United States' involvement in this war led us to immigrate to Canada in order to bring up our children in what was, at that time, a more peace-loving nation. A few months after the reunion with my father we moved to Nova Scotia. Isa promised he would visit, but the distance was too great. Once in a while he telephoned. There would be awkward pauses in our conversation, for in actuality we had very little to say to one another. So much had taken place in our separate lives that it was impossible to catch up.

The books he had sent me remained on Ema's bookshelves. As I could no longer read Estonian easily, it seemed pointless to take them with me when I left. Unopened and untouched, pristine, each one bearing my father's carefully composed inscription to the darling daughter he had seen so seldom, they were eventually discarded along with most of the other mementoes of our past lives.

Memories become more precious as we age and have more time for reflection. I wish I had those books now.

31.
Fellow Travellers

My mother travelled better at my age
than I do at hers.
I unravel easily.
And though I pick up the stitches,
I am not as tightly woven.

"I DON'T THINK SO," Ema says. But I am sure. I recognize the windows on the ground floor, the front door and the three stone steps.

It is 1998. We are in Tallinn, on Rosencrantz Avenue, scrutinizing a four-storey, pale-yellow apartment building made of stone. The courtyard has been paved over, and cars, mostly Ladas, are parked where the sandbox used to be.

"Of course it is," I contend. "Don't you remember? That's the window Memme called me from."

My mother is eighty-five. I am fifty-nine.

We are tourists, foreigners in what used to be our homeland. Ema is wearing a smart-looking polyester pantsuit, her waist trimly belted, her hair styled in a grey bob. I tower over her, my feet in sandals under my ankle-length cotton-print skirt, my wispy ash-blonde hair pulled back into a dishevelled knot.

We walk a bit further and come to an empty lot covered by a profusion of wildflowers protected by a fence. A building used to stand here. The rubble has been removed. It is a memorial.

Plaques along the fence display a message in various languages: Estonian, Russian, German, English: TALLINN WAS BOMBED BY THE SOVIET AIR FORCES DURING THE EVENING AND MIDNIGHT

OF MARCH 9, 1944. 53 PERCENT OF LIVING SPACE WAS DESTROYED. 20,000 PEOPLE LOST THEIR HOMES. 463 PEOPLE WERE KILLED AND 659 WERE WOUNDED.

Our memories of that night are doubtless quite different, my mother's and mine. We don't share them, just stand there silently together.

When Ema first invited me on this trip, offering to pay the round-trip fare from New York to Tallinn, I said no. I hate to travel. My breathing gets shallow, my bowels undependable, my palms sweaty.

"Thousands of people fly every day. Why do you consider yourself so important, Tita, that you think the plane you happen to be on is the one that will crash? I'm offering you this chance so you can begin to appreciate your heritage. You might learn something. But if you don't want to go, well, of course that's up to you."

The tone of her voice said everything, and I understood perfectly.

It wasn't only because of my fear of flying. I don't like road trips either. There are others who exhibit the same symptoms, and a label legitimates our deficiency: *Separation Anxiety*. I couldn't reveal to anyone that what I dreaded even more was the thought of spending ten days alone with Ema, who would be in charge of this trip from beginning to end, controlling my every move. Still, I had to be mature about the opportunity. Ema invited me and offered to pay. I was hardly a child. My own children had grown up and moved away. I had stopped teaching the year before. My time was my own. My fears were ephemeral, imaginary, psychotic. I had to go.

By investing her savings wisely, Ema had accumulated a sizeable bank account. When she retired from the prep school at sixty-five and had to vacate her apartment, she purchased a condominium in town. Never idle, she soon established a reputation in the community as a formidable bridge player and a commendable watercolour artist. Her floral paintings were promoted by a local gallery, which sold everything she produced.

"And at a good price too! I can hardly believe it," she exulted with typical Estonian modesty.

During the winter months, she took courses at the Community College, mostly in art, but since they were offered free of charge to senior citizens, also in many other subjects that captured her interest—geology, poetry, architecture. In addition to her annual trip to Nova Scotia to visit us, she travelled to places she had always wanted to see—Hawaii, the Caribbean, England, Norway, South America—and in 1992, shortly after the liberation from Communist rule, to Estonia.

The first journey back to the land which they fled from fifty years ago turned out to be a considerable disappointment for almost anyone who was able to make the trip when Estonia was finally free. They should have waited a few years. They had been too eager. After the constraints of Soviet occupation, the country remained in the throes of extreme poverty, and there were very few facilities to accommodate the large influx of expatriate Estonians coming back for a visit. Ema was hoping to reconnect with the remnants her family. Since the mid-fifties she had sent packages and corresponded regularly with her mother. Although Memme lived well into her eighties, it wasn't quite long enough.

On this first trip back, she did see her brother Oss and met his family. They had never been close growing up. *He always ran with a different crowd,* she told me, curling her lip to make it obvious what kind of crowd it was, and her opinion of him remained the same. The photograph she showed me later depicted two old people staring unsmilingly into the camera.

"He took everything from our apartment after we left. He even has my photo albums," she complained.

"Why didn't you ask for them?"

"He never offered to give them to me."

"Maybe he felt resentful of your wealth and your foreign ways," I suggested. And your readiness, as always, to voice your opinions, I thought but didn't say. It seemed understandable to me why those who remained behind enduring the Soviet regime would feel some antagonism toward the rich émigrés returning fifty years later to criticise and give advice.

"Why do you always have to be so negative, Tita? You must realize that without overseas dollars, very little can be accomplished there."

By 1998, when we went to Estonia together, the facilities had indeed improved. My mother was right—a great deal of money was contributed by Estonians from all over the world to help in the reconstruction. Businessmen especially took advantage of the many opportunities afforded by an emerging nation. In less than a decade of new independence, Tallinn had become a Mecca for tourists.

And that's what we were. Though we could speak the language, we were strangers in what was essentially a foreign land. We knew no one. After being notified of her brother's death, Ema had no further contact with his family. When I suggested she at least get in touch about getting her photo albums back, she was evasive. She didn't have their telephone number. They were probably away for the summer, in the country.

"But surely they wouldn't mind giving them to you if you asked," I insisted. "I'd love to see pictures of you and my father when you were young. And of me when I was a baby. And so would your grandchildren."

"I would have asked for them before, if I knew they meant anything to you," she sniffed. "But you never showed any interest in your heritage."

It was quite obvious that the rift was permanent.

Ema had rented a lovely apartment for us in the centre of Tallinn, owned by a wealthy Estonian couple who lived in New York. It was late spring. Lilacs bloomed everywhere and filled the air with a nostalgic scent. Street vendors sold hand-knit woollens and bouquets of spring flowers. A beggar played familiar folk songs on his accordion. Surrounding the large city square, restaurants overflowed with people eating and drinking on patios. Each day we strolled along the ancient, narrow walkways crowded with other sightseers, stopping in innumerable small shops and outdoor markets to examine the merchandise and to buy souvenirs. Ema pointed out where she was brought up on Narva Avenue; where she went to *Gümnaasium*; where she had walked down the cobblestone streets with her girlfriends and stopped to gape at Volli's picture in the store window; where, as a young woman, she had a job in an architectural firm.

The day after our arrival, we boarded a streetcar to Kadriorg Park, an elaborate garden designed in the eighteenth century by Peter the Great for his bride Katherine. We took pictures of the swans in the lake and of the nearby buildings—the Tsar's castle (converted into an art museum), the President's residence painted pale pink, the famous sculpture *Russalka* commemorating lives lost at sea.

"I used to take you on walks in your carriage in this park," Ema remarked. "But of course, you wouldn't remember that."

In the evening, we attended a performance of *Swan Lake* in the rebuilt "Estonia" theatre, walking back to the apartment through rowdy groups of Finnish tourists who regularly took the ferry across the Baltic Sea to indulge in the strong and cheap Estonian beer. Even Ema forgot where she was at times and began to order a meal or speak to a clerk in English, for modern commerce had made its inevitable inroads all over the world. We ate in restaurants serving foods that had become familiar to us, with no Estonian dishes on the menu. A MacDonald's stood at the gateway to the medieval section of the city. If the ancient ruins had not been so meticulously restored, we could have been anywhere.

It was very easy to separate the people one saw in the city into three distinct groups: Tourists, native Estonians, Russians. Immediately after the occupation, the Communist government built massive housing projects for the Russian workers who thronged into the newly annexed country, eager for jobs. Mostly these were uneducated peasants looking for a better life. The countryside was still marred by the large ugly constructions built for workers when private property was nationalized.

In 1991, when Estonian once again became the official language, nearly a third of the population was unable to speak it. This led to enormous social and political pressure and dissension. The Russians, after living there for more than a half a century, wanted to stay, but the Estonian majority was against assimilation and was attempting to use all of its political savvy to force the Russians out, a conflict which has still not been satisfactorily resolved.

Our first few days in Tallinn had progressed smoothly. We were both making an obvious effort not to let petty annoyances upset us. The fourth morning after our arrival, however, as we were sitting at the sunny kitchen window, writing postcards and eating the traditional Estonian breakfast of black bread, cheese, sliced ham, and strong coffee, Ema happened to mention that anyone who had owned land in Estonia before the Communist takeover in 1944 could now apply to get it back.

"Too bad we were city dwellers, eh?" I joked.

"The Otts were landowners," she said. "They had a large farm in Rakkvere County. Their older son, Madis, has applied."

"Oh?" I said, surprised. "Is he planning to move back to Estonia?"

"No, of course not. Though he did marry an Estonian girl and his children know the language. He's an engineer, as you know—or perhaps you didn't—and he makes a lot of money. He has a beautiful estate in West Hartford, and he also owns a cottage in Maine. His children and grandchildren live nearby. I'm sure he wouldn't want to move that far away from his family. Most people don't."

I should have been warier, perceiving the critical implications to my own meagre achievements. But I was only half listening, busy enjoying my bread and cheese and writing a message home.

"What about the other son?" I asked to continue the conversation.

"He doesn't want it. He didn't apply. They got into quite a row about it and no longer see each other unless it's absolutely necessary."

"Who owns the farm now?"

"It was taken over by the Russians."

"So a Russian family has worked the land there for over fifty years, and now Madis is going through all sorts of rigmarole and red tape to claim it as his. Doesn't he have enough? I could understand, maybe, if he really wanted to move back to the old homestead, or even if his children did. But he's a wealthy man who has established his life in another country. Whether they're Russians or not, these people have lived here for a lifetime. Now because of some stupid government decree, it suddenly belongs to someone else. He'll be an absentee landlord, just like the German nobility was a hundred years ago."

"That land belonged to his grandparents."

"The land he owns now belonged to Native Americans," I responded, slurping my coffee. "Though they never did take much stock in private property and felt that land was communally owned by all creatures on the Earth. Madis has everything he could possibly want. Why does he need more?"

"Don't you understand anything, Tita? The Estonian government is doing all it can to get the Russians out. We may be too small to go into battle with the Russian Bear but we can outsmart him."

I should have heeded her exasperation but, regressing back to my adolescent perversity, I continued on.

"That Russian family has worked the land too, and they have been in Estonia longer than the Otts have lived in America. They raised their children here, and their grandchildren. You mean to say the government is going to force them to leave their home because some rich American says he is the rightful owner? Where will they go? What will they do? Why can't people just try to get along and forgive each other? Two wrongs don't ever make things right."

"You, of all people, should know better, Tita."

Her tone startled me enough to look directly into her face. She was livid, her head waggling in indignation.

"You are an Estonian yourself, though you've always preferred to deny it. You have no respect for your heritage or the sacrifices your ancestors have made so you can have a better life. You only think of yourself. *Pfui,* Tita. What are you, a Communist?"

It was the worst insult in her vocabulary.

And you, Mother, are a Fascist. You have no compassion for those who are different from yourself. You detest the Russians, the Jews, the Catholics, the Muslims, the Blacks, the atheists, the liberals, the gays, people on welfare, unwed mothers, and all those who are brave enough to speak out against war, repression, and the injustices they see in the world. You think only Communists promote propaganda and that the platitudes spoken by those with whom you agree are the truth. You have always hated the part of me that is not you, and I have always detested your superior attitude. I should have said all this long ago, but I've tried to protect your feelings since you are my mother, and, as you so often reminded me over the years, you are the only one I have and you have only me.

True to my nature, I didn't vocalize any of that. What I said was nothing, sitting mutely with my mouth open, letting the import of our polarity sink into my consciousness. I was talking people; she was talking politics. I was feeling sorry for individuals; she was vindicating her country. I was talking peace; she wanted victory through manipulation because it was impossible to win a war against such a powerful enemy as Russia. I went to the bathroom to take a shower and got dressed, and we continued the controlled and superficial relationship that we had maintained throughout our lives, knowing that the only thing that had ever brought us closer together was distance.

It was fortunate that Minna, an Estonian woman from Connecticut whom my mother knew slightly, was also visiting Tallinn and happened to be staying at a hotel directly across the street. Ema had arranged for us to meet, and the diversion of other people couldn't have come at a better time. Minna had many relatives in Estonia, and, along with her two younger cousins, we all took the streetcar to Piirita Beach.

Unlike the rough rocky shore of Nova Scotia, the Baltic Sea appeared like a vast lake. Again, it was the smell that brought back the memories—the feel of gritty sand between bare toes as I filled my red tin bucket and turned it upside down to miraculously create a torte; sitting astride my father's broad shoulders, clutching tightly to his hair as he walked far out into the deep water; flying high on the big chair swing, safely tucked between my parents; dancing at the pavilion while the orchestra played "When Mickey Mouse Went Out to Sea;" sunbathing naked next to my mother in *Naiste Paradiis*. Yes, I had been here before, though all that was gone now. The tall pine forest remained, and the constant gentle lapping of the small waves.

To commemorate the occasion, I had brought a moon snail shell from the shores of Nova Scotia to place on this beach that was so special to me in childhood. It looked immense and lavish among the miniature shells of the Baltic Sea. Yet I left it there, thereby disturbing the purity of the region but perhaps also providing a thrill to someone who might discover this giant aberration.

What compelled me do this? I wonder. Was it an attempt to create continuity through a metaphor only I could possibly comprehend?

The next day, Minna's relatives were nice enough to include Ema and I on a road trip in their old Lada to view the farmhouses, windmills, and small fishing villages of rural Estonia. We stopped for lunch at a feudal manor that had been transformed into an expensive hotel, before touring the magnificent ruins of an ancient monastery razed by Ivan the Terrible in the sixteenth century. I took a lot of pictures, discovering later that all of these sites were represented much more effectively on postcards.

On our last night in Tallinn, we attended an outdoor concert in the large amphitheatre originally built for the annual song festival. Now, what we heard there was rock and roll and I felt a great nostalgia well up inside me, not for the country where I was born but for the one where I had grown up—America. Only then did I fully apprehend what Ema and Isa and all those others had lost so long ago. Their youth. The romance, music, passion, idealism, those wonderful dreams and hopes for the future, that apex of elation and despair between being a child and becoming an adult that can never be recaptured but resonates for a lifetime. They were displaced persons. Their most vibrant recollections remained in a time and place that had vanished forever.

For over fifty years as exiles, the people of my parents' generation strove to recapture their former identity in foreign lands: the Estonian church service held once a month in various borrowed facilities; the choral group recalling forgotten melodies; the aging folk dance troupe trying to recruit younger members; the patriotic orations by geriatric freedom fighters to celebrate the first Independence Day; the social circle made up only of other Estonians; the parties and dances to encourage the young people to mingle with their own; the school on Saturday mornings for the little ones to keep the language alive; the Estonian newspaper published in New York that arrived once a week.

Do you remember her, Totsu? Ema would write, mailing me yet another black-bordered obituary of some Estonian who had recently died, cut out from "The Free Estonian Word." *We were in Laager together.*

Though scattered widely throughout the western world, the first generation of refugees were united by a spirit of avid nationalism. Our homes reflected a devotion to Estonian tradition by the prominence of pillows, rugs, book covers, and photo albums, as well as items constructed from wood, leather, cloth, and silver, all featuring ethnic designs. Paintings and photographs depicted Estonian landscapes. Reproductions of Tallinn's famous tower, *Pikk Herman*, flying a miniature Estonian flag, sat on our tables and bureaus. Roped silver chains and round brooches bearing Viking ships or heraldic crests were worn as costume jewellery. Pickled herring, black bread, *rosolje*, and *kapsa pirukad* were offered to guests. Birthdays were celebrated with both *torte* and *kringle*. *Kalevipoeg*, the Estonian national epic, had an honoured place on the bookshelf.

But time and distance erode the power of ethnicity. It is nearly impossible to keep a culture thriving in exile. People pass away, people change, new people are born. What was once reality might be looked upon with interest and nostalgia, but is no longer an essential part of one's daily life. Despite enormous odds, most people my age married other Estonians and kept the old traditions alive. For their children, however, this inclusive and obsessive nationalism could no longer be sustained, and, when Estonia did once again become free, the most devoted patriots were too old to return. Those who made the trip found that life there was no longer the way they had envisioned. Even the language had changed. What we had so doggedly preserved had become stagnant, the speech of *Auslanders*. Ema was as much of a stranger in Tallinn as I was.

A nation split apart for so many years can never fully merge again. Those who left will remain *Auslanders* forever. Though we may visit often, especially if there are family connections, we don't stay long. Whether we like it or not, our lives are now established elsewhere. We have homes, gardens, careers, children, pets, and friends, and a new extended family speaking another language with different customs and interests. Inevitably, despite parental disappointment, Estonian is rarely understood in the homes of the third generation. It is now no longer the responsibility of exiles to preserve the old culture and traditions. After all those years of Communist repression, Estonia is free once more, and the people who remained there will carry on.

All my life I had thought us the lucky ones to have escaped the horrible oppression and poverty of Communist rule. But during our visit, one of Minna's Estonian cousins said something which astounded me: "We always felt so sorry for you refugees, leaving all you had behind and going off into an unknown world. It was hard for us here too, there's no doubt about that, but at least we were home."

What I brought back from our trip, in addition to a few souvenirs, was a deep sorrow for the losses that had been endured by so many and a full realization of my own rootlessness. Ema had always regretted the fact that I had no real home. And I discovered that she was right.

32.
Ema in Her Later Years

MY MOTHER NOW LIVES in a seniors' residence. I visit her once a year. Ema is ninety-four; I am sixty-eight.

For many years we have both been conscious that when I leave, this goodbye might be our last, as with any parting from anyone. Maybe I am more attuned to this than most. That is why I hate to travel, for I always fear that I might never be back. Yet I continue to brace myself to make the yearly trip to see her because she is no longer capable of coming to see me.

We have come from a place where we can never really return to a place where we will never truly belong. Yet because I was transplanted when I was still a child, a large part of my life has had a cohesive progression that was forever denied to my mother and father and to the millions of others who have been driven out by war from the land of their birth. The songs I danced to in high school are still played on the radio as oldies but goodies. My photo albums record the important events of my life. My friends and my family surround me. I can pass on my treasured possessions and property to my children and grandchildren. My intellectual development has not been irrevocably curtailed or hampered by suddenly having to begin life anew in a foreign land with a different language after my formal education was completed. Playing Scrabble with her grandchildren, my mother still begs for special privileges because English is not her native language. *But you spoke it for so many years before we were even born,* they complain. *Besides, you always win.*

In actual fact, Ema became more assimilated into American

society than most of her contemporaries, mainly because she was able to get a position commensurate to her education and abilities. In her later years, having outlived all of her former Estonian friends, one could say she became Americanized herself.

Isa, on the other hand, kept his patriotic fervour to the end. He was an Estonian man, an Estonian soldier. He fought for his country. He had been willing to give up his life for it. He continued to be what he was when he was young—a consummate romantic. He died in 1989, two years before Estonia regained independence. Perhaps it was better that he was never able to go back for a visit. He loved his fatherland with the same idealistic vision that he regarded the daughter he hardly knew, a love that can be sustained only through absence.

Soon after we returned from our trip, Ema was diagnosed with *myositis*, a debilitating muscular disorder. At the time, it manifested itself only in a slight shaking of her head and a weakness in her left hand, but since it was a degenerative disease, she decided it was time sell her condominium and rent an apartment in a senior residence while she was still capable of living unassisted.

My mother was always a perfectionist—her bureau drawers tidy, underwear and stockings neatly folded, her important papers carefully filed away, her inner self orderly and under control. Confusion, sloppiness, multiplicity of meaning, the differing and unique interpretations of the human condition had no place in her life. *Work hard and you shall succeed, Totsu, and if you don't, work harder.* To her I remained the child who floated thither and yon upon the waves, or jumped over them, or rode them to shore, while she put on her bathing cap to swim her strong breast stroke through the turbulence into the calmer sea on the other side.

Since her move to the residence, we devote at least one day during my annual visit to reorganizing her large closet, crammed with clothes that span the decades.

"I have too many," she complains.

"You just have to get rid of an item that you no longer wear whenever you get something new," I advise.

But when faced with the actuality of discarding anything, she balks.

"I bought that on sale, but it was very expensive. Oh, what the heck," she says. "Put it in the back where it was. Just in case."

The outfits she wears most often we hang accessibly in front, her sweaters and jerseys on the shelves above, arranged by colour.

"Fold it neatly now, Tita," she orders, "not like that."

It takes her ten minutes to show me how, smoothing out the wrinkles with her crippled hands.

Some things she tries on, but everything still fits. Although shorter in stature than formerly, she has remained slender all her life.

Her eyesight is failing. "Are there spots on this?" she asks. "Throw it in the wash, please. Over there."

"This is a bit nubbly, but I can still wear it for exercising. Put it in the back. No, not with the suit. On the other side."

"And that blouse? I know it's got a big stain that won't come out, but the collar is nice. It looks good under my white sweater. Put that over there too."

Her collection of cashmere sweaters is kept in a special drawer.

The heavy winter clothes are stored in the communal storage room in the trunk labelled FOSTER CENTER, RHODE ISLAND, U.S.A.

By evening we are both exhausted. There is a small bag of items that I have convinced her to give to Goodwill. Her closet resembles a painting, an abstract landscape: the shelves in graduated hues of blues, purples, greens, and yellows, ascending from dark to light; the trousers, which she now prefers to skirts, hanging stiffly by their creases below; her shoes lined up in a straight row along the floor.

"Thank you Totsu," she says. "A job well done. Now, what shall I wear to dinner?"

She selects a lavender cashmere sweater, grey slacks, and silver jewellery. Since the dining room is usually quite chilly, she takes along the raw silk shawl that her globe-trotting granddaughter sent from Thailand.

"Ready to roll," she announces, and although she can still get around with a walker, it takes too long, so she takes her "chariot" instead. Making sure her door is locked, she speeds down the long hallway to the elevator in the motorized wheelchair she recently acquired because we can't be late for our five-thirty sitting.

Dinner is an elegant affair. There is a choice of appetizer, salad, entrée, and dessert. Also wine. I have two glasses. She has one to keep me company. The facility provides many part-time jobs. Young people—high school and college students— serve. They have been instructed to be patient and cheerful.

"This is my daughter," Ema introduces me to anyone who happens to pass by our table. "She has come all the way from Nova Scotia, Canada."

"Your mother is amazing," they comment. "And what a bridge player! She always wins."

Ema smiles and nods, not hearing what is said unless the person speaks directly to her. The world of the senses, the outer environment, has become increasingly blurry.

The parts are wearing out, but the motor still works, she says good-naturedly.

Yet she prefers the challenge of taking care of herself rather than asking for help. She still manages by ingenuity, by *kombineering*. Flat on her back, she pulls out the table with her feet to accommodate the extra leaf when she is having company. She fastens her zippers with a paper clip and buttons up with a crochet hook. For a half hour each morning, she does exercises to strengthen her muscles, her aged legs pumping the air. She styles her own hair because it looks better than when the hairdresser does it. She has sold her ancient car (a much younger *Blue Baby*) to an Estonian girl for $100, not because she thinks herself incapable of driving, but because her insurance premiums are so ridiculously high she refuses to pay them. After many months, we have finally convinced her that it isn't a good idea to drive without insurance, despite the fact that she's never had an accident.

Recently she has also sold a painting of lilacs she just completed, her last one, she insists, but I don't believe it. As she no longer has her car, she drives "the chariot" six blocks, crossing four lanes of traffic, to have her nails done.

"Don't they have a manicurist in residence?" I ask.

"Of course they do," she replies, "but not a good one."

We have survived into the new millennium.

Coda

THE FINAL PHOTOGRAPH I received from my father depicts an old man, impeccably dressed in a white shirt and grey cardigan, sitting on a bench outside a train station. One large, strong hand—I remember how little mine felt in his—is striking a match to light his pipe. A small boy sits beside him, clutching at his arm and gazing into the distance, the two-year old son of his other daughter, his real daughter, the one who shared his life.

This young man, my father writes in Estonian, his familiar fanciful script shaky now, *is waiting with his Taat for the "too-too" to bring his Mamma home from Chicago. Since he comes to our house nearly every day while his mother works, he is learning to say words in Estonian. When we were still together, you also spoke like this: Pappa goes away on the "too-too" to fight Stalin. Perhaps you remember?*

I don't. How could I? My memory begins at three. But he remembers. He has kept a little girl, his first daughter, within the frame of his consciousness. In one of his final telephone calls, he remarks that since the distance between us is too great for an old man like himself to travel, he would prefer to wait until he dies to see me again. It will be easier then, he says.

His strength already waning, his health declined rapidly after his son, my half-brother, was lost in a tragic drowning accident, and he died not long after.

And eventually he does come, as he promised he would.

My half-sister always pursued our family connection. Although both she and her brother had visited once in Nova Scotia, I was reluctant, even afraid, to establish a close relationship. We kept in touch, but barely. I had my mother and she had me. That was enough. Thus it truly is amazing that our children, never having met, living in different countries, born more than a decade apart, have found each other as adults, becoming not only long-lost relatives but also close friends. Thirty years later, we gather together to celebrate the wedding of this same little boy in the photograph. Despite all the impediments, we have finally joined as a family.

It is during this ceremony that I see my father again. Not as he was, but as he used to be, standing straight and tall, with his bright gaze looking toward the future. Isa, before he was defeated, before we became refugees, when he was still a young man in Estonia, shouting KRAMBAMBULI and throwing me up into the air. I cannot stop the tears which stream down my face, knowing full well that what I am seeing is no supernatural apparition but my sister's beautiful twenty-one-year-old daughter, born after my father died, who bears his face and stature with feminine grace.

Despite time and distance and even death, our lives remain connected. *He loved you so much*, his other daughter wrote when she informed me of our father's death, *but he was never very good at showing it.*

My mother I always knew intimately—aware of her long, manicured fingernails; her sharp, evaluating eyes; familiar with her bathroom habits, her smells, the personal noises she made, the filth and beauty of her existence that was never revealed to anyone else. We have been attached, each to the other, longer than to anyone else in the world. Though we may become stuck in our own version of the story, I know you Ema, just like you know me, from the inside out.

Often she still wants to say to me: *You will always be Tita.* But she restrains herself and says instead: *Think of your cup as half full, not as half empty, Totsu,* which is even more irritating. An indomitable, exasperating woman who does not realize that the positive attributes she instilled in me have nothing to do with her exhortations. From her I learned how to replenish my cup, so that it is hardly ever half empty—although she is still reluctant to accept that we never preferred the same sort of brew. As the years pass by, both of us have made a conscious attempt to appreciate each other's strengths and forgive what we perceive as weaknesses. It has taken a lifetime, but sometimes she allows me my own opinions, and I have to grudgingly acknowledge that hers have not always been wrong.

We speak now mostly of poetry.

For the past several years, three Estonian women of my generation meet with my mother once a month to share their translations of Estonian poems into English. There is a luncheon, followed by wine, chocolates, readings, and an inspired discussion at Ema's exclusive literary salon. I am an *ex officio* member, sending my contributions by e-mail. Although my mother never did take to the computer *and now it's too late,* she laments, one of the other club members prints out and reads my translation to the group. We all take this task seriously, aware of the beauty and power of language, both Estonian and English. We have come to realize how difficult it is to convey ideas and feelings through metaphor and image while making the words flow like music. According to the Estonian custom, there is always much self-denigration of one's own efforts while praising that of others.

Ema is ninety-nine. Her muscular disease has so crippled her that she can no longer bend her fingers to use a pencil or pen, so she types her translations on an old electric typewriter. Legally blind due to macular degeneration, she uses a magnifying machine so she can read her work to me on the telephone. Slowly. Line by line. We discuss certain words and phrases.

"Is this better? What do you think, Totsu?"

"Yes, definitely," I say.

"No...." She considers. "I like the way I had it before. It's closer to what the poet really meant. Don't you think so?"

"It's very good, Ema, as usual."

"Posh," she replies, pleased. "Yours is much better. It takes me so long to do everything. The parts are wearing out, but the motor keeps on running."

As elderly ladies, we both make the effort to look upon each other with generous eyes. Yet there are still moments of suppressed conflict, and if we spend any amount of time together, we inevitably fall into established patterns.

When she mentions that all the other people at the residence have their families living nearby, I feel guilty, which I am sure is the intent.

When she says, *I realize now I didn't bring you up well*, what can I possibly say in response?

When she says, *Of course you have a wonderful relationship with your children*, I don't take her to mean that I am a good mother, but that I am a bad child.

When she says, *You're doing so well with all your interests*, I feel as though she's implying I'm living my life in a rehabilitation centre.

But then again, as she says, I am overly sensitive and shall be until I die.

She always regretted that I never had a "normal" life—*noormalne elu, Totsu, that's all I ever wanted for you*—and I have wished the same for her. But it could never be for either of us—the typical family with its wonderful joys and inevitable sorrows, that ephemeral ideal, which cannot really be defined or even pointed to among acquaintances, for we all have our singularities. Yet everyone seems to know exactly what it is, for it glows like an illusory beacon of home. For those who have experienced abuse, it is nearly impossible to achieve, as the tentacles reach far inside and are unforgiving. For people abused by war, it takes several generations to fully recover.

I had a dream once, so vivid that for a moment I was unsure whether it was in fact real, something I had perhaps forgotten as people do when they become older and events begin to disappear from the screen of their consciousness. Ema was in a relationship with a man who cared for her, who held her hand, who touched her hair and gazed with obvious tenderness into her eyes. They never married, but they went out to dinner and to the theatre; they walked in the sunshine and travelled to distant lands; they made love. My mother seemed so different, a woman pampered by someone other than herself, full of an inner joy she had never possessed except perhaps when Onu Gusti was with her. At that time, my eyes were filled with fear and jealousy, and I did not see clearly. Since then, she put aside any man who may have entered her life and I have borne the burden of her love. I am the guilty one. As a young child I guarded her with the entire strength of my being so that she would not leave me for another, before transforming into the neglectful daughter who left her mother alone all these long years.

"You are the only one I have," she says sometimes even now, when she's feeling sorry for herself, before she realizes this is no longer true. Although we all live at great distances from one another, she has three grandchildren and a great-grandchild she has driven around on her lap in "the chariot" showing her off to the other residents.

Pfui, she says. "The world is not like it used to be. Everything is sex and violence these days."

"There was enough violence during Stalin's and Hitler's time, I respond, and probably plenty of sex as well."

"That was different," she says. "That was war."

Would *we* have been different, Ema and I, if war hadn't disrupted our lives? Most assuredly. But we were fortunate to survive and to have a lifetime to recoup, to make the best of what we had. No one except her knows the entirely separate world inside me that exists in a different language and time. I am grateful now to still be able to say those simple words fraught with the magic of childhood:

Kodu – home
Ema – mother
Isa – father
Onu – uncle
Tädi – *aunt*
Piim – milk
Leib – bread
Talu – farm
Head aega – literally translated as "good times," meaning farewell or goodbye.

And it might come to pass that if I speak any last words in the delirium of my deathbed they will be in Estonian, my mother-tongue, which none of my loved ones will understand.

Head aega, Ema.
Head aega, Totsu.
Good times.

Ema died suddenly in the summer of 2015 after completing her evening exercises. At the time of her death, she was still living independently at the residence, with her mind as sharp as ever. She was one-hundred-and-two. Our last conversation took place a few hours earlier and dealt with the fine points regarding our latest poetry translation. Of course, we disagreed.

Author's Note

Although the names have been changed, this work is based on facts as perceived through the eyes of a child. Memory is selective and others may view things differently.

I would like to thank Inanna Publications for publishing this book.

Photo: Cress Baker

Syr Ruus was born in Tallinn, Estonia, during the Second World War. As a small child, she escaped with her mother to Germany and subsequently immigrated to the United States where she earned an MA in English, an MS in Education, and taught briefly in the English Department of Illinois State University. She moved to Nova Scotia in 1968 where she worked as an elementary school teacher while raising her three children before devoting herself full-time to writing. Her short fiction has appeared in anthologies and journals. Her 2006 novel, *Lovesongs of Emmanuel Taggart*, won the Writer's Federation of Nova Scotia H. R. (Bill) Percy Prize. Since then, she published three books of fiction inspired by the South Shore of Nova Scotia: *Devil's Hump* (2013), *The Story of Gar* (2014), shortlisted for the Ken Klonsky Novella Award, and *In Pleasantry* (2016). Her novella, *Walls of the Cave,* is forthcoming in 2019.